FORWARD TOGETHER

FORWARD TOGETHER

SOUTH CAROLINIANS
IN THE GREAT WAR

Edited by Fritz P. Hamer

Charleston   London

History
PRESS

Published by The History Press
Charleston, SC 29403
www.historypress.net

Front cover: Patriotic artwork from the 1919 *Garnet and Black* yearbook. *Courtesy University of South Carolina Archives.*
Back cover: Image from Mexican border service; the Second South Carolina Band just finished playing "Somewhere a Voice is Calling." *Courtesy Robert L. Brown.*

First published 2007

Manufactured in the United Kingdom

ISBN 978.1.59629.244.4

Library of Congress Cataloging-in-Publication Data

Forward together : South Carolinians in the Great War / edited by Fritz Hamer.
        p. cm.
  Includes bibliographical references.
  ISBN 978-1-59629-244-4 (alk. paper)
1. South Carolina--History--20th century. 2. World War, 1914-1918--South Carolina--Influence.
3. Soldiers--South Carolina--History--20th century. 4. University of South Carolina--History--20th century. I. Hamer, Fritz.
  F274.F67 2007
  975.7'043--dc22
                                            2007006808

Notice: The information in this book is true and complete to the best of our knowledge. It is offered without guarantee on the part of the author or The History Press. The author and The History Press disclaim all liability in connection with the use of this book.

CONTENTS

PREFACE

For three years the continent of Europe had witnessed the world's most destructive war where millions of men perished on battlefields across northern France, Belgium and Eastern Europe. Until April 1917, Americans stayed out of the fray, in part because of the age-old advice of George Washington, more than a century before, that the nation should stay out of international conflicts. It was also President Woodrow Wilson's wish to remain neutral. First elected to the nation's highest office in 1912, in his second run for office four years later Wilson declared to the electorate that he would keep the nation out of the international conflict at all costs. Although he seemed sincere in this sentiment, he would soon be compelled to change his mind. With foreign trade increasingly threatened by German U-boat attacks on the high seas, more and more Americans began to think that their freedom to trade across the globe was threatened. And most were sympathetic to the British and French sides. The American president and his cabinet held similar sentiments. As we know, they finally joined, declaring war on Imperial Germany and her allies. Some of the reasons for this went back to the closer cultural bonds of a common language and style of government that the United States had with Britain and France. Perhaps even more important, although muted at the time, were the much larger investments of American businesses and industries with the Western powers, to the tune of $2 billion for the French and British but only $20 million for the Germans and her allies. It has been argued since the end of the Great War that many in the United States could not risk losing this huge investment if Britain and her allies lost.[1]

When President Wilson declared war on Germany and her allies, South Carolina was one of his staunchest supporters, along with most Southern states. And for the Palmetto State there was more than just patriotism motivating its native sons. In some ways the state was still recovering economically from the effects of the Civil War. The infusion of federal money that the national war effort would bring had important economic ramifications for nearly every community and farm in the state. This potential motivated many businessmen and politicians across the state to lobby for military installations. This patriotic zeal combined with economic self-interest is demonstrated in the chapters by Fritz Hamer and Krissy Dunn. Men and women from Greenville to Charleston supported the new installations by setting up canteens, hosting dances and joining the nurse corps to aid recruits. Of course, along with the benefits that came with these installations there were problems. Community leaders worked with military officials to find solutions to overcrowding, lack of transportation and health problems that the influx of recruits and their dependants brought. But even when there were local protests over these issues, they rarely significantly disrupted the state's contributions to the war effort.

Elizabeth West's analysis of the University of South Carolina shows how one of the state's most significant educational institutions maintained a semblance of its mission while supporting the war. Although many faculty left to serve in the military or assist with wartime logistics elsewhere in the state, classes continued. To augment the dwindling male student body that went off to war the president of the university permitted more women to become students, increasing this segment of the student body significantly.

As housing and food shortages and some health issues caused problems for many communities in some sense, these were minor compared to the other changes that war brought. As Jason Shaiman demonstrates, the federal government's campaign to garner support across all levels of society instituted a new kind of national control never witnessed before. Under the auspices of the U.S. Committee of Public Information, each state was expected to make sure that all its citizens loyally supported America's war effort.[2] As shown by Shaiman and Hamer, those citizens perceived to be disloyal (whether real or imagined) faced severe penalties. The normal recourse to legal defenses often disappeared in the war emergency. Governor Richard Manning and his State Defense Council demanded complete support and were unwavering in using any means possible to stamp out pockets of "unpatriotic" individuals. If the thousands of Four Minute Men sent out to communities across the state could not induce total patriotic support then every means possible was permitted to eradicate perceived disloyalty. If public pressure failed to convince some citizens of the need for unfettered patriotic zeal then the state resorted to legal authority and emergency decree to make South Carolinians comply. Such measures seem a common thread throughout twentieth-century wartime emergencies up to the current crisis in the early twenty-first century. However, in each emergency, whether in World War I or the present war on terror, use of government authority and legal means too often leads to an abuse of power and denial of legal rights of many innocent citizens.

As for those South Carolinians who fought the war in the trenches overseas, more than three thousand who entered the armed forces distinguished themselves, whether fighting the Germans directly or supporting the front lines with essential supplies and food. Soldiers and marines who were not in combat brought up supplies, built roads and gave comfort and aid to the wounded. Joe Long shows how South Carolina troops performed "over there" and highlights some of the most distinguished units from the Palmetto State. Men from the 30th Division were in the thick of the fighting and a few earned the nation's highest honor for bravery under fire. Unlike today, the American Armed Forces were segregated and African American units were often put into labor roles behind the lines. But some, such as the 371st Regiment, distinguished themselves on the front lines, although fighting under French command. Their remarkable story and those of other South Carolinians are revealed in Long's chapter.

By the time the fighting ended and the troops began coming home the state, with the nation, had changed. The thousands of soldiers and marines who came through South Carolina for weeks, often months, of training brought new economic opportunity to the citizens of the state. Many natives interacted with Northerners and Westerners for the first time and began to see that many were not all that different, even if they spoke a "little funny." New relationships were created by the war that often blossomed into long-term ones that would not otherwise have happened. But while the strain of war waned quickly, the one thing from the past that persisted after 1918 was segregation and second-class status for African Americans. Despite the heroic service they gave to the war effort, both at home and abroad, whites refused to recognize them as full citizens once peace returned. The inroads to Jim Crow laws and customs made during the war largely disappeared, but a hint of change was in the wind that would steamroll into massive social transformation in forty years.

The Great War had opened the eyes of South Carolinians to new economic and social opportunities, but for the state to fully realize them would take many more years. I hope that you will find this small volume on South Carolina's role in World War I an interesting account that will lead you to further inquiry.

Fritz P. Hamer
Curator of History
South Carolina State Museum

ACKNOWLEDGEMENTS

Ninety years ago the United States declared war on Imperial Germany and its allies, the first time in American history that the nation intervened in a European conflict. To commemorate this anniversary and the Palmetto State's history during this momentous period, several cultural institutions in Columbia have collaborated with each other to develop complementary exhibitions, a website and this catalogue. To find out more about the exhibitions and related programs check the website: www.scforwardtogether.org. The authors of this brief study wish to thank The History Press and its editorial staff for their invaluable assistance in producing this work, with special thanks to Jenny Kaemmerlen and Hilary McCullough.

Seeds of Change: World War I, South Carolina, Impact and Contributions

Fritz P. Hamer, South Carolina State Museum[1]

In January 1919 Catherine Ravenal, superintendent of the Ladies Benevolent Society of Charleston, submitted her organization's 106th annual report. Although it had 166 members, only 35 actually attended the annual meeting. Not surprisingly, their leader had glowing things to say about the aid it had provided to the city's poor during the previous year. The society had collected hundreds of cans of food and dry goods, provided supplies and financial support to a nurse and her aides and had seen only one of its clients die from the flu epidemic that had gripped the state and the nation just weeks before, even while its nursing staff attended to 117 cases. Fortunately it appeared that all the cases, save that one, had recovered or were recovering. But while the precarious health of many of the city's citizens appeared much improved from the fall, Charleston would never return to the society it had been prior to 1917. Until then, Charleston and the entire state of South Carolina had remained largely an isolated state with only marginal economic and political ties to the nation at large.[2]

One could say that this change was brought to the Palmetto State by one of its own, for President Woodrow Wilson, who led the country into the Great War in April 1917, had spent a portion of his youth in Columbia. After resisting those who wanted the United States to enter the war during its first two years, the president changed his mind and took the nation into war with a fierce idealism to spread American democratic ideals and a slogan made famous that this was a "war to end all wars." Although this idealistic slogan seemed sincere, it is unlikely that he envisioned the social and economic changes that it would garner for many Americans, including South Carolinians. For the first time since the Civil War a half-century before, women would have new opportunities in the workplace rarely dreamed of in peacetime. Similarly, the nation's African Americans would have chances to experience broader options in both the workplace and society. Although neither group held onto their wartime gains following the armistice in November 1918, it gave both women and minorities a glimmer of what they might have in a more equitable society when social restrictions and segregation laws were finally abolished. The war became a seed for change whose full impact would take four more decades to realize. Other sectors of Palmetto State society were also affected. The depressed farming communities of the state began to break out of their lethargy that had persisted almost since the Civil War. Expanding battle lines overtook European fields left fallow by farm boys gone off to war. The shrinking food production there left an opening for American farmers. Likewise, South Carolina's most lucrative cash crop—cotton—revived as Western nations' needs for new military uniforms and ordnance needs (artillery shells needed cotton) grew. Although the farm economy of 1910 struggled to make any kind of profit, five years later it suddenly grew robust, and farmers across the state and the South began making more money than they had in decades.[3]

Although the economic fortunes of farmers and other Americans had begun to improve even as the nation tried to maintain strict neutrality in the conflict, most

Student Army Training Corps, Presbyterian College, Clinton, South Carolina, 1918. Campuses across the country formed these units during the war to prepare them for military service. *Courtesy Presbyterian College Archives.*

Americans sympathized with the Allies, especially Britain. South Carolinians largely mirrored this sympathy and as the war stretched on this support became more explicit. As German U-boats intensified their attacks on Allied shipping, sympathy for Britain and her Allies increased. Such incidents as the May 1915 sinking of the luxury liner *Lusitania* in the Irish Sea intensified this support, in large part because more than one hundred American passengers lost their lives. In 1916 South Carolina Governor Richard Manning told the federal government that his state would support the establishment of an armed militia, part of a bill Congress entitled Armed Neutrality. One of the first steps made by a then-reluctant Wilson to prepare the nation for a possible conflict, many in the nation still considered this a timid response. At the beginning of the new year, when unrestricted submarine warfare was declared by the Kaiser's government, relations between the United States and Germany grew more precarious. The infamous Zimmerman telegram became the final straw in this tense relationship. This February 1917 incident stemmed from a German diplomatic blunder when a document sent by Berlin to Mexico City was leaked. Germany offered Mexico a deal: the Southwestern United States for an alliance with the Central Powers.[4] While such a scheme seems preposterous and it appeared that the Mexican government never seriously considered the proposal, Congress was outraged. President Wilson asked for a declaration of war and four days later, on April 6, 1917, Congress overwhelmingly approved the request. Congress's majority opinion was reflected in South Carolina at least a month before war was declared. In March 1917 the *State* newspaper in Columbia declared, "If the United States is to survive as a self-respecting republic honorable among peoples of the earth, she must put on her armor. When the rest of the world is at war we should be strong enough to look with serenity upon the plottings of desperate government and their ministers."[5]

A few days after this editorial, University of South Carolina students demonstrated their support for war preparations when they pleaded with the university president, William S. Currell, that he and the university trustees accept military training for the student body. Less than a week later they did. Similar feelings were voiced around the rest of the state. In April the *Greenville News* praised the president, who "has set forth the position of the United States, making it clear that this country will not permit Germany unmolested to sink its ships, murder its citizens" or conspire against its sovereignty.[6]

Charleston's city fathers backed the war, no doubt helped by the aborted sabotage scare in their midst. The German freighter *Liebenfels* was impounded in the port of Charleston soon after war broke out in Europe in 1914. On January 31, 1917, its skeleton German crew sank the freighter in a failed attempt to block the channel to the navy yard a few miles up the Cooper River. But not everyone in the state condemned the action.[7]

Although patriotic sentiments were widespread in the state, a few voices spoke out against war, even in Charleston. Irish Americans of Charleston, led by sometime mayor and newspaper editor John P. Grace, opposed any support for England in its war with Germany. As many Irish Americans across the nation continued to do, Grace remained a fierce supporter of Irish independence and spoke out often in Charleston and elsewhere

---

John P. Grace (1874–1940)

Born in Charleston of Irish parents, Grace became a lawyer who first ran for mayor in 1911. After his election Grace directed further park construction, championed health legislation and improved rail access to his city. Defeated for reelection, in part because of his political opposition to Governor Richard Manning, Grace founded the *Charleston American* newspaper in 1916. This became Grace's mouthpiece to criticize both Manning's administration and Wilson's war policy. As an Irish nationalist, he opposed any alliance with Great Britain, even after the nation entered the war. However, in order to prevent the government from shutting down his newspaper for fomenting "sedition" against war, Grace stepped down as editor in fall 1917. After the war he ran another successful campaign for mayor, where he continued to champion improvements in city life and its local economy.

---

against British oppression of his ancestral homeland. Grace's antiwar editorials in his *Charleston American* clearly delineated his opposition to war fever. Just before Congress voted for war Grace published a letter to the editor that accused the war hysteria of being something "instigated by Wall Street gamblers and munitions manufacturers who desire very much to hand over the cash money in the United States Treasury...to the Allies so that they will be able to pay their war debts."[8] The state's most vocal critic of note was former Governor Coleman Blease. The reactionary leader argued that the nation had no business getting itself tangled in European affairs that to him had little import to the United States. Coupled with these vocal critics of war, there were sizable German ethnic communities in Lexington, Charleston and Newberry Counties. Although these enclaves had existed since before the American Civil War, some maintained their ethnic roots with pride and were reluctant to go to war with their ancestral country. Charleston even had a German-language newspaper, *Deutsches Zeitung*, that continued to publish until anti-German feelings forced it to shut down in late 1917.[9]

But not just German-language papers were curbed. The *Abbeville Scimitar* kept up a constant attack on the war even after the nation became involved. Its editor and publisher, W.P. "Bull Moose" Beard, an ally of Coleman Blease, wrote brutal, often racist editorials opposing war not so much on moral or political grounds, but on baser instincts. In one May 1917 editorial Beard warned that all white men should oppose the war because it presented a grave threat to white supremacy. He based this on the supposition that if blacks had to be saluted by white men, how would the former be expected to return to the cotton fields at the war's conclusion? He concluded, "I wonder if the old pine tree at the baseball park would hold them all if that bunch of sassy nigger preachers had made such talk at the courthouse here." Laced with such diatribes, Beard became the target of federal and state authorities in summer 1917.

By November 1917 Beard was convicted of sedition and imprisoned, and his paper shut down.[10]

Yet African Americans, the state's largest ethnic group, strongly supported the president's call to arms. Even so an initial surge of black volunteers for the military within weeks of the declaration of war was not received enthusiastically. In fact, Governor Richard I. Manning declined to accept African American volunteers to the state's national guard, instead urging them to return home and support the war through greater diligence on their farms and financial support through Liberty Bond purchases and other forms of financial assistance. Manning, like other white authorities inside and outside South Carolina, feared that such an influx of minority volunteers might cause problems for the military, not to mention reduce the labor needs of farmers and others throughout South Carolina. Rumors surfaced that African Americans might be infiltrated by German spies who would "subvert" black soldiers in the United States. Such fears had no basis in fact. During spring 1917, the nation's foremost black leader and editor of the *Crisis*, W.E.B. DuBois, declared in no uncertain terms that such anxiety on the part of whites was preposterous, and that even if German agents tried to subvert black recruits it "would not for a moment have been considered." Nonetheless, only white volunteers were accepted into the military until the draft began in earnest in late summer. After that large numbers of both races entered the military with patriotic zeal. Unlike many white troops, most African American units would see little combat on the Western Front, instead serving in logistical units bringing up supplies and building or repairing roads to the battle lines when they arrived in France (see chapter four for details on exceptions to this general rule).[11]

White fears of possible black insurrection had originated generations before, when many planters and other whites feared slave insurrections. Though such antebellum anxieties were often exaggerated, in 1917 many whites still viewed blacks as threatening. Despite white suspicions, African American leaders such as DuBois, founder of the National Association for the Advancement of Colored People less than a decade before, encouraged blacks to show their loyalty to the government and contribute to the war effort in any way they could. For it was DuBois's contention that once peace was achieved blacks would finally receive equal justice and assume their rightful place in American society that had been so long denied to them. He put this in stark terms to his readers in May 1917 when he wrote: "Bad as it [war] is, slavery is worse; German domination is worse...Enslaved, raped and despised though he [the African American] has been and is, the Negro knows that this is his country because he helped found it, fought for its liberties and ever upheld its ideals." In South Carolina one of the major leaders of the minority community was Reverend Richard Seymour. Although much more accommodating to whites than DuBois ever was, he traveled across the state advocating support for the war through Liberty Bond purchases and encouraged young men to enter the military once Uncle Sam called. He received heightened prestige in both the black and white communities of the state. Most African Americans, inside South Carolina and beyond, accepted the call to arms with patriotic zeal. According to one source, black draftees exceeded whites

Poster announcing Reverend Richard Seymour's presentation in Pineland, South Carolina, 1918, a prominent African American leader from Columbia. Notice that, despite strict segregation laws of the day, at this event whites were encouraged to attend with blacks (albeit in a separate section) to hear his speech. This is one of the few state-produced posters that has survived. *Courtesy South Carolina Department of Archives and History.*

in the Palmetto State by 7,500 and made up nearly 53 percent of the total number of military-age registrants.[12]

Although DuBois and Seymour's hopes for a postwar America proved unfounded after the armistice, there were few who disagreed with their leaders' arguments at the time. Most South Carolinians, regardless of race, eagerly wanted to do their part for the war effort. Spurred on by headlines that the war was a crusade "For Liberty and Humanity," Governor Manning appealed to all citizens of the state to contribute to the war effort through any means possible.[13] Many enlisted in the armed forces, but opportunities abounded for those who could not. Women in Columbia began organizing canteens for soldiers training at Camp Jackson, while others did the same for camps in the Upstate and on the coast. Other groups organized women's committees for the Red Cross to make and collect clothes, aid the sick and provide meals to soldiers on and off their bases. At home South Carolinians were encouraged to support the federal government's national voluntary program for food conservation. To support this citizens were encouraged to grow gardens in any empty plot they could find; some were even motivated enough to plow up parts of their own yards. Enthusiasm for this program reached all levels of society. In the Greenville County mill village of Piedmont one local leader observed at the end of August 1917 that nearly every family had raised twice as many fruits and vegetables as they had the previous year. Canning increased to preserve the surplus. Although such fervor made citizens of the state feel like they were doing their part, it is difficult to gauge how much this actually helped the war effort.[14]

As the state and nation prepared to train an army for operations overseas, the Palmetto State became a major center of instruction for new soldiers, sailors and marines. Two camps were established in the Upstate, on the outskirts of Greenville and Spartanburg. The largest center in the state was Camp Jackson in the Midlands, on the eastern outskirts of Columbia. On the coast the small Charleston Navy Yard began to suddenly grow into a significant installation for training sailors and constructing medium and small warships. It had taken nearly two decades since its move from Port Royal for the city fathers to finally realize their dream for the naval installation. The former navy yard on Parris Island became the marine corps training center for new recruits in 1915 and once Congress declared war it quickly expanded into a larger, bustling center.

Each training center became a small city unto itself that included mess halls, barracks, movie cinemas and parade grounds. To construct these camps required huge amounts of supplies and men, something demanded in many other places throughout the nation. Consequently shortages caused delays and forced young trainees to pitch in amidst their military training to help with construction. In addition, government and military officials sometimes had difficulty bargaining with landowners on some of these issues. While most owners were eager to lease or sell property for a new military installation, others were less enthusiastic.

Camp Jackson, outside the state capital, had both promoters and detractors. The campaign to bring a military installation to this city began months before Wilson asked Congress to declare war. Eager for the social and economic stimuli that the camp would bring, city fathers and business leaders worked hard both at home and in Washington to bring the army to the Midlands. To make it more attractive, the area chamber of commerce collected $50,000 from its members to acquire options on land where they thought the camp would go. In April 1917, one of Columbia's leading businessmen, Edwin Robertson, purchased rights to one thousand acres between Garners Ferry and Old Camden Roads. A month later Major Douglas MacArthur announced in Washington that Columbia had been chosen as the site of one of sixteen national "cantonments." By the time an armistice had been signed at least 200,000 soldiers had trained there.[15]

The camp's construction began soon after the official announcement and continued through the late fall of 1917. In mid-June the army's supervisor of construction, Major William Couper, arrived to oversee the work and left a detailed impression of daily activities, now deposited in the South Caroliniana Library. By the end of June two thousand men were intensely working to erect the buildings of the new camp. Although recruits began to come in by the fall, Couper did not officially turn the camp over to the U.S. Army until January 1918. During this period he spent nearly $8.9 million, half of it in wages to laborers working ten-hour days. To accomplish their assignments these workers used 5,748 carloads of materials, more than half of this lumber, and another 2,340 carloads of supplies. Initially told to build a camp for thirty thousand men, the army revised this to forty thousand soon after Couper arrived. He was also ordered to build stables and corrals for 12,247 animals. Further expansion continued during

Camp Jackson under construction, 1917. Such scenes were typical of other installations being constructed elsewhere in the state and the nation. *Courtesy South Carolina State Museum.*

construction so that the federal estimates put the total cost of the project at $12 million. By the time of its completion Camp Jackson had 1,554 buildings on 2,237 acres amidst the sand hills of the Midlands.[16]

But Couper had to manage more than just the camp's construction. Although he had to deal with employment issues that ranged from plumbers wanting more pay and shorter working hours to workers who used scarce roofing material as raincoats, he also had to deal with other issues outside the construction zone. Perhaps his biggest headache was preventing rival construction firms from luring his workforce away to other federal projects. He also had competing interests who disagreed about salaries for the workforce. One local congressman pestered him to raise workers' wages while Frank Hampton, local landowner and business leader, wanted him to pay less. Hampton argued that field hands were happy to get one dollar a day but were now getting four dollars as carpenters only because they could saw a board "without missing the line more than an inch or so." Hampton also haggled with Couper over rights of way and drainage of swamps near his property.[17]

By the middle of the summer more than ten thousand workers hammered, sawed and raised new buildings and built roads at a steady rate. On weekends this workforce transformed Columbia into what Couper called "a mining town compared to what it [had been] six weeks ago." By October Couper took pride in his creation; for him Camp Jackson looked like a city that had always been there. And in many ways it truly was a

city unto itself. It had its own road and rail system, bakeries and stables, along with an airfield, a balloon detachment and an officers' training school, to mention just a few things. And this was just what city fathers had dreamt of when they began lobbying in late 1916. After the war, the *State* observed that without Camp Jackson Columbia would still be a poor, struggling Southern town. But instead, "scores of merchants and other businessmen now are on solid ground, whereas a little while ago those not cramped in their operations by lack of capital were few and far between."[18]

Similar tales, albeit on a slightly smaller scale, could be told for the other camps and naval installations that blossomed in the Upstate and the Lowcountry. Greenville's leaders hoped to attract a military installation prior to the declaration of war and on their own took out an option on one thousand acres on the northeast edge of the city. In June 1917, when General Leonard Wood came to the Upstate city at the invitation of the chamber of commerce to see the site, he announced that a camp would be

Some of the hundreds of workers employed to build Camp Jackson, 1917. *Courtesy South Carolina State Museum.*

Top: View of a portion of Camp Jackson, circa 1918, where more than 200,000 soldiers were trained for battle in the trenches of the Western Front. *Courtesy South Carolina State Museum.*

constructed on the outskirts of Greenville. Prominent local families leased two thousand acres where the railways went through. Under the direction of Major Alex C. Doyle, army quartermaster, who arrived in July, work began. Instead of wooden barracks the new camp was to house its recruits in tents with wooden flooring. Unlike Camp Jackson, designated a national army cantonment, the army built Sevier as a national guard training camp. Consequently it had fewer permanent buildings and covered less acreage.[19]

Under Doyle's supervision the Fiske-Carter Construction Company, with military and civilian engineers on hand, began to clear land, lay out streets and level the land for drill fields. The new installation became officially designated Sevier in honor of the renowned Revolutionary War militia leader and governor of Tennessee, John Sevier. Before construction ended thirty thousand recruits had arrived and begun their training. With the influx of men from throughout the Southeast and beyond, Greenville had new economic opportunities that greatly improved the community's business and social activity. New demands for entertainment and restaurants added to the opportunities for local businesses. One notable family business that received an important boost was that of Mrs. Harry C. Duke. She prepared thousands of sandwiches for the camp's canteens using her own mayonnaise recipe. After the war she perfected this and began to produce her special sauce commercially. Although bought out in 1929 by C.F. Sauer of Richmond, Virginia, he continued to operate the

The souvenir cover of a Camp Sevier booklet. This cover was generic; every camp in the nation used the same picture, and only the name of the camp was changed. Soldiers often purchased these to send home or kept them to remember their training. *Courtesy South Carolina Room, Greenville County Public Library.*

Greenville factory and use the Duke name that remains prominent on supermarket shelves today.[20]

Only a few miles east, Spartanburg also attracted its own national guard training facility. Announced at the same time as the one in Greenville, this camp was located three miles west of the city center. And as in Greenville, the Fiske-Carter Construction Company carried out most of the clearing and construction. When completed in fall 1917, it had more than fourteen hundred buildings, including hospitals, mess halls, recreation halls and stables. In addition, miles of sewage pipelines and new roads had to be installed to accommodate the influx of recruits.[21]

By early October the first large contingent of troops came in from New York, one of its national guard units now designated the Twenty-seventh Division of the U.S. Army. In part to honor the new division's home state, the army designated the installation Camp Wadsworth, after the Union general of the Civil War. A native of New York, Wadsworth died of wounds suffered at the Wilderness in 1864. The Upstate town not only was filling up with New York soldiers but also their families, many of whom followed their loved ones to training. Spartanburg, with a peacetime population of twenty-six thousand, was slow to accept so many newcomers at once, especially since it lacked sufficient housing for such an influx. Sometimes friction ensued between the locals and troops, but generally the community slowly adapted to the changes after a period of adjustment. Nonetheless, residents of the Upstate city were accused of raising rents and demanding exorbitant prices for lodging and food. One local landlord who

A wagon team at Camp Sevier, perhaps bringing equipment or other supplies through one of the camp streets. *Courtesy South Carolina Room, Greenville County Public Library.*

normally had charged $150 per month suddenly told her tenants that the fee would be doubled because she had been offered this by one tenant. For a while local grocers and other merchants reportedly charged military personnel up to 50 percent more for food and other items. After the military began boycotting some businesses that were singled out for profiteering, camp authorities met with the local chamber of commerce to devise a table of prices that were then published in the local paper. In this manner locals and military alike could determine which businesses were charging too much. By publicizing this, most merchants quickly learned that it was bad for business if they tried to charge more than others. Besides conflicts over prices, in some cases the New York troops found Spartanburg to be annoyingly "small-town," lacking the variety and vitality of large cities they were used to. Such attitudes from outsiders led to local resentment, but both sides adapted for the remainder of the division's stay.[22]

But one event that nearly led to a bloody riot occurred in fall 1917, when the U.S. Army ordered a regiment of Northern black troops for training in the Upstate camp. When the Fifteenth New York arrived in Spartanburg most residents were shocked. Efforts by the local chamber of commerce to dissuade the army from its intentions, once they learned of the order, failed. Despite one representative warning that "it is a great mistake to send Northern Negroes down here, for they do not understand our attitudes," army leaders thought differently. The mayor of the town told a *New York Times* reporter at the same time that they would be treated just as blacks in South Carolina were and that he saw nothing but trouble if the order was carried out. Although the white officer in charge voiced similar misgivings on sending his troops to Spartanburg, he carried out his orders and moved his regiment to Wadsworth. Within a few weeks, tensions between locals and the New Yorkers became palpable, spurred on, in part, by the August riots in Houston. There, another black regiment had become enraged by the local population's racist abuse. After several incidents they broke out of their camp in a rage, killing seventeen civilians and wounding many more. Soon after the Fifteenth New York arrived, biracial groups of soldiers had confrontations with white businesses in town, some of which led to fistfights and near brawls. Then a white truck driver nearly precipitated another Houston-style riot. He told some black soldiers that two of their number had gotten into a fight with some local police. After the soldiers were overpowered, the driver claimed the police hanged the two in the police headquarters yard. Later, when the two individuals in question did not report for roll call at the camp, forty members of the regiment armed themselves and headed for town in search of their companions. Fortunately, before the angry group reached their destination their white commander got wind of their actions and raced toward town to forestall them. After their commander, Colonel William B. Hayward, took some of the group's leaders aside to review the police blotter, they quickly discovered that their comrades were not even listed. Reassured that no one had actually been hurt or executed, the soldiers came to attention, shouldered their rifles and marched back to camp. Ironically, citizens of the town who were unaware of the reason for the unit's actions saw the troops marching back in good order and applauded them. Soon after this near-tragedy, army commanders

Joseph H. Harbin, one of thousands of natives from South Carolina who came from Lebanon, South Carolina (in Anderson County). Drafted in fall 1917, he probably was at Camp Sevier until his unit, the 118th regiment of the 30th Division, left for France in spring 1918. *Courtesy South Carolina State Museum.*

One of the tent streets of Camp Sevier, probably done when the street was preparing for an inspection. A similar scene could have been found at Camp Wadsworth, circa 1918. *Courtesy South Carolina Room, Greenville County Public Library.*

realized their order had been a mistake and the Fifteenth New York was ordered to France to avoid another possible incident.[23]

Wadsworth trained not only recruits, but nurse cadets as well. One of the first camps of its kind in the nation, the graduates of this school became invaluable to the troops both at Wadsworth and overseas during the conflict. Just as important as the nursing school, the camp needed an area to train its artillery units. For this it needed land more remote than Wadsworth. Consequently, isolated property was rented in northeast Greenville County in the area of Hogback and Glassy Mountains. Covering an area ten miles long and three miles wide, this mountainous locality served as training grounds for hundreds of artillery units learning to fire large guns. Thousands of rounds of ammunition were scattered there for more than a year. When training in this remote locality the soldiers set up a tent sub-camp outside Campobello and Gowansville that provided more economic opportunities for the local farmers and small businesses in the area. Not only did businesses prosper, but this sub-camp also gave people chances to interact with nonresidents, most of whom were from New York. For many it was their first encounter with "Yankees" and most found the experience much better than they had expected. Thus while the remote area reportedly had old residents who had fought at the Wilderness and Appomattox under General Lee, they were curious to see U.S. Army troops in their midst wearing "butternut jeans" like regular workmen, instead of the blue uniforms with brass buttons that they were used to fifty years before.[24]

While the Midlands and the Upstate hosted training centers for the U.S. Army, the Lowcountry provided significant support to the U.S. Navy and the marines. Although the navy had maintained a presence on the coast at Port Royal since the Civil War, this began to change at the dawning of the twentieth century. Through the political maneuverings of Senator Ben Tillman and other members of the South Carolina delegation, the small navy yard at Parris Island had moved north in 1901 to a base ten miles up the Cooper River from Charleston. While Tillman's intent had been to garner more political support from the Lowcountry constituency that never had favored him, the economic prosperity that he hoped the new installation would give the city had not materialized.

The nearly abandoned Port Royal continued to be the base for a small contingent of marines until 1915, when the navy decided to move its recruit training center from Norfolk, Virginia, to the former navy base. Soon it would provide a variety of local jobs and new businesses to the Beaufort/Port Royal area that flourished until after the 1918 armistice.[25]

Although the new navy yard's first dry dock was completed in 1909, the Charleston facility did not produce its first vessel until 1916 when the navy tugboat *Wando* slid off its shipping ways. Within less than a year the slow progress of the facility would change radically. The first hint that the nation was on the verge of war occurred months before

The U.S. tugboat *Wando*, coming off the shipping ways, Charleston Navy Yard, 1916. This was the first vessel built at the yard; prior to that time the facility had refitted existing ships in the navy. *Courtesy South Carolina State Museum.*

the U.S. Congress declared war on Germany. Officially neutral when war began in 1914, U.S. authorities impounded the German merchant vessel *Liebenfels* and her small crew at the South Carolina port. When the dispute with Germany over shipping rights and unrestricted submarine warfare heated up in early 1917, the officers and small crew who remained on *Liebenfels* decided that they should hinder the U.S. war effort by scuttling their vessel in Charleston Harbor in an effort to block the channel. The attempt failed and several of the crew were convicted of illegally trying to block a navigable river and sentenced to prison terms. In the meantime the German vessel was re-floated, brought to the navy yard and refitted as an armed cargo vessel renamed *Houston*. Thus began the navy yard's wartime duties, refitting captured enemy vessels and constructing other smaller navy ships for the duration of the war.[26]

As the fledgling navy facility became a bustling center of ship construction and reconversion it also developed into a training base for new sailors and a manufacturing hub for naval uniforms. After employing just a few hundred men up to the outbreak of war, the facility expanded rapidly into a workforce of more than five thousand, along with naval personnel. Converting four more German merchant vessels brought from other U.S. ports, the yard also converted a German battle cruiser captured in the Philippines that was brought to Charleston. The yard also constructed several gunboats, tugs and other smaller vessels for the U.S. Navy. According to one postwar account, the facility constructed thirteen new vessels and repaired over two hundred others, both American and Allied. In addition to ship construction and refitting, the facility had the

Shipbuilding cranes A and B at the Charleston Navy Yard, 1916, just before major activity began to transform the facility. *Courtesy South Carolina State Museum.*

U.S. Navy's only uniform plant. While 90,000 garments were produced in 1914, this grew by 3,000 percent to 2.7 million four years later. By the end of the war this plant alone employed one thousand women.[27]

Along with producing ships and uniforms, the navy yard also trained new sailors in various specialties. By the end of the war about twenty-five thousand men had received training ranging from machinist skills, radio, signaling and lead and compass work, along with basic marching drills and boating skills. Perhaps one of the most distinguished sailors to be stationed at the Charleston Navy Yard was the artist Norman Rockwell. Although he ended up in the South Carolina coastal city by accident in 1918, he was soon discovered by the commanding officer of the training center, where his artistic talents were quickly employed; first on the yard newsletter, *Afloat and Ashore*, as a cartoonist and, more than a few times, to paint the portraits of many officers and enlisted men.[28]

With so much activity going on inside Charleston, it seemed an appropriate target for German U-boats to target to forestall its contributions to the national war effort. Fortunately for the citizens and naval personnel of the coastal center, this never happened. Although rumors abounded that U-boats had sneaked ashore for supplies and brief rest, the navy never could verify this. However, it would not be difficult to imagine enemy incursions on the South Carolina coast after Rear Admiral Frank Beatty's scathing report in fall 1917. The admiral castigated the nearly defenseless nature of the coast in and around Charleston. Nearly six months into the war, the commander of the reconstituted Sixth Naval District, headquartered in Charleston, reported to superiors in Washington that his command consisted of only three small, armed vessels and two unarmed minesweepers. He still lacked mines and submarine nets and had no means of convoying anything anywhere. All his men could do was "scout" the U-boats if they showed up. Either Charleston was too small for Germany's attention or the Kaiser's submarines were too sparse on the high seas to pay the coast of South Carolina any attention.[29]

The German navy's lack of interest was appreciated farther down the South Carolina coast at Port Royal Sound, where the recruit center for the U.S. Marine Corps had expanded. Based on Parris Island, the recruit depot began to formally train new recruits in late 1915. Using the structures left by the navy, the island began to grow significantly once war was declared in April 1917. Unlike today, Parris Island was only accessible by barge or boat during World War I. This provided the marine drill instructors (DIs) with the perfect kind of isolation to mold their new recruits into the fighting men they needed for the Western Front. Most new marines went through a grueling eleven-week training schedule during World War I that saw about forty-six thousand new marines prepared for combat.[30]

For nearly two centuries Parris Island had been the center of plantations and small farms where sea-island cotton had been the major cash crop. Although the island continued to be the residence of a few small farmers through the 1930s, the island steadily became marine property until the last farmer left before World War II. Massive new construction early in World War I saw the small naval station grow into a 160-acre cantonment costing $4 million, with two other smaller, semi-permanent camps.

The first became known as the Maneuver Ground, where up to four thousand men at a time lived and trained. The other was the rifle range, where recruits learned marksmanship and other specialties of firearms. By the early spring of 1918 there were approximately 233 temporary buildings erected west of the current parade ground that housed five thousand men and another two thousand who had to use tents. On the Maneuver Grounds, at the isolated southern portion of the island, several mess halls, a hospital and other outbuildings were built near a tent city where four thousand recruits lived and trained at one time. Men remembered later that hours of drill and instruction were punctuated with road building. One former marine remembered spending half the day in "weapons training and endless marching, the other half was spent in building oyster shell roads. Nights were spent battling sand fleas." In the summer the heat and humidity were often excruciating. Throughout the war the Maneuver Grounds and the other two training areas were a beehive of activity, producing new marines for the fight in the trenches of France. To keep pace with all this new construction and provide adequate support an electric light plant, expansion of the post bakery, post office and ice plant occurred during the war. The bakery alone produced five thousand loaves per day. To connect all this new construction with maneuver areas and firing ranges, miles of new roads were constructed largely with tons of crushed oyster shells.[31]

Applicants for enlistment arriving at Paris Island

To reach Parris Island new recruits had to take a boat from the mainland. A causeway was not built until a decade after World War I. These new marines usually remained in their civilian dress until several days after arriving. *Courtesy Parris Island Museum, United States Marine Corps.*

To occupy the moments during camp life when recruits had a break from military training, every effort was made to keep them occupied with other activities. Among the most popular for recruits and officers alike were athletic contests that training centers from Parris Island to the Upstate encouraged. The most popular were baseball, football and boxing. Regular competitions were held in each camp with leagues, and on occasion they would play teams from the local communities near which they resided. In the summer of 1918 the baseball league for marines on Parris Island had some high-scoring affairs that included former Major League players. Forty-fourth Company's team pitcher was Paul Cobb, brother to future Hall of Famer Ty Cobb and a former professional with the Cleveland Indians. Although he appeared to be a bit rusty, giving up thirteen runs, his team backed him up with twenty-eight more to win the game. Other Major Leaguers also joined the corps and contributed to the baseball leagues of the island. Jack "Dots" Miller, former captain and first baseman for the St. Louis Cardinals, and "Nig" Clark, former catcher of the Cleveland Indians, played on teams during the war years.[32]

Football proved popular as well. At the Charleston Navy Yard there were several teams made up of sailors and marines and on occasion they would schedule games against army units in the area and a few civilian teams in Charleston. These other squads came

A roomy bunkhouse and good beds await them on arrival

Inside one of the barracks at the main northern end of Parris Island where the navy yard had been. Only a portion of the marine recruits' training had the luxury of such facilities; often they lived in tents when they trained at the Maneuver Grounds or the rifle range. *Courtesy Parris Island Museum, United States Marine Corps.*

from The Citadel—South Carolina's military college in downtown Charleston—soldiers stationed at Fort Moultrie and even teams of marines from Parris Island. Sometimes competition became too intense. In one football game a sailor died from head injuries received in a heated contest at the yard near the end of one match. Nonetheless, despite the occasional tragedy like this, the commandant of the Naval Training Camp, Commander Mark St. Clair Ellis, wrote in his Commander's Policy of 1918 that among many duties that a sailor needed to know, from how to defend oneself with a rifle to rowing a boat, he also needed to know how to play baseball and football.[33]

While athletic events were popular, they were not the only outlets for recreation and entertainment for the troops. Every training center had at least one band that often performed both at the camp and in the community near which they were stationed. At Camp Wadsworth the band held concerts, parades and teas that drew hundreds of civilians. With such large numbers of men from all walks of life, professional actors, as well as former Major League ballplayers described above, could also add to the entertainment of camps. From Wadsworth, a budding playwright from Princeton, Lawton Campbell, wrote a musical play entitled *Swat the Spies* that was performed in Spartanburg's Cleveland Hotel. The lead role was played by Private Cornelius Vanderbilt Jr. And along with such drama there were dozens of dances held weekly at every base that local women organized and military

Left: Recruits on Parris Island drilling with bayonets in a simulated trench. *Courtesy Parris Island Museum, United States Marine Corps.*

Below: A boxing match on Parris Island. In World War I boxing was very popular across the nation, just as much as baseball and football. *Courtesy Parris Island Museum, United States Marine Corps.*

bands played in. This gave troops the opportunity to meet the local gals, which, on occasion, led to romance and marriage.[34]

As South Carolina did its utmost to provide space and entertainment for an influx of military recruits, its citizens did many other things to contribute to the war effort. Farm production, which had begun to rise before 1917, accelerated after April 1917 as the nation called on all its farmers to produce food not only for its citizens but also for its Allies who were in desperate need. Although this enabled farmers to make profits, many for the first time in decades, it was difficult because manpower was in short supply. Nonetheless, crop production rose significantly during the war years. From 1912 to 1916 the average annual income from crops had stood at $121 million. By 1918 this had risen nearly four times to $446 million. While some of this increase was due to inflationary pricing, it still gave many farmers huge profits. And even while Americans were not deprived in any appreciable way, food czar Herbert Hoover asked everyone to give up voluntarily certain staples once a week. Consequently it became fashionable within a few months of U.S. entrance into the conflict for communities in South Carolina and across the nation to have meatless Tuesdays, wheatless Wednesdays and porkless Thursdays, along with two dessertless days per week. In addition, by summer 1918, certain foods were rationed, especially sugar. Starting July 1, each person was limited to three pounds of sugar per month, which led to ice cream producers having their sugar allotment reduced to 75 percent

YMCA dance, possibly in Columbia, circa 1918. Note U.S. and French flags in the background. *Courtesy South Carolina State Museum.*

of the normal consumption and soda makers even further, by 50 percent. This naturally affected other food producers of things such as cough drops, beer, honey syrups and vinegar. But while it was an inconvenience, it hardly amounted to a major sacrifice of one's well-being.[35]

But perhaps the most popular contributions made by South Carolinians to the war effort in direct economic terms were the purchase of Liberty Bonds and war stamps. From nearly the moment that war was declared in April until a few months after the armistice, a year and half later, newspapers had almost daily remonstrances to their readers to buy bonds to finance the Allied war effort. To strengthen people's commitment (and overcome reluctance that others might have), rallies were held in communities throughout the state. The financial support (and public display) that this provided were important enough to state and federal officials that even at the height of the flu epidemic in fall 1918 (when all sorts of public gatherings from church services, schools and theaters were suspended), rallies to sell bonds continued in Charleston, Columbia and Greenville. The total contributions by the state's citizens by the end of the war came to $120 million.[36]

In Greenville three major Liberty Loan Drives were held, the first in June 1917. As in this and the two subsequent ones in October and the following year in April, citizens of the town enthusiastically supported the drives with regular contributions. Interestingly, in the first drive more than half the goal of $750,000 was met by mill workers, some of the lowest-paid members in the community. Likewise the black community enthusiastically got behind the April 1918 drive by forming a Colored Committee consisting of leaders who met at a local Baptist church to decide on their strategy for raising money within their community.[37]

In Columbia the black community proved their enthusiasm for the cause by contributing a considerable sum to the Liberty Loan Drives. During the second campaign of 1917, African Americans of the Midlands purchased

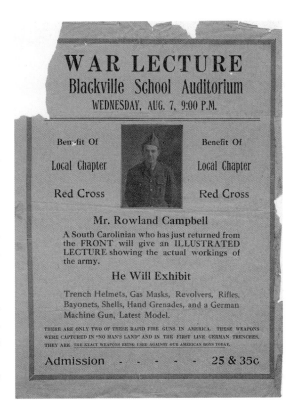

Poster announcing a lecture on the Western Front by an American veteran, August 1918, Aiken, South Carolina. Such lectures were another way to bolster support for the war. *Courtesy South Carolina Department of Archives and History.*

Bernard M. Baruch (1870–1965)

A native of Camden, South Carolina, Baruch became one of Wilson's key advisors on the economy before and during the war. Initially appointed to the president's Business Advisory Board in 1916, after the declaration of war, Wilson selected him to be a member of the War Industrial Board (WIB) and later its chair. Many say that Baruch was the brains behind the mobilization of American industry for the war effort. Having gained fame and fortune on the New York Stock Exchange at the turn of the century, Wilson and his cabinet sought his advice and council as the war clouds mounted. Baruch lived and worked mainly in New York City, but in 1905 he purchased seventeen thousand acres in Georgetown County, where he often spent time and hosted many national and international dignitaries before and after World War I.

Bernard Baruch at his South Carolina coastal retreat in Georgetown County shortly before World War I. *Courtesy Belle W. Baruch Foundation.*

bonds worth $45,000, which they topped the following year by acquiring $50,000.[38] Elsewhere in the state black communities matched, and perhaps even surpassed, this level. In Greenville the editor of the local paper remarked that black citizens of the city had done so much for the war effort by June 1918 that their patriotic efforts should be an example for its white citizens, who loved to voice their patriotism "but who will not give a cent to provide for the welfare, comfort, and happiness of our soldiers overseas." Although most of these contributions were in small amounts, a few people in the minority communities raised large sums. Such was the case for J.J. Atwell, a black insurance salesman and captain of Richland County's third bond drive, who personally raised $6,150.[39]

Most communities throughout the state did their best to outshine everyone else. Charleston made one of the largest claims. As in most major towns and cities, military parades were used to kick off each new Liberty Loan Drive. This was what helped to boost sales among citizens in each community. At war's end Charleston's Chamber of Commerce claimed that its citizens raised $21.1 million in five loan drives, a fifth of all funds contributed by the Palmetto State. Whether these numbers are completely accurate or not, Charleston's enthusiasm for the war effort, as shown in this boosterism, was matched in many other towns and cities throughout the state.[40]

Yet there were plenty of events that occurred during the nation's brief wartime experience that almost dampened this enthusiasm. As noted, there were a small number of South Carolinians who opposed entrance into the European conflict, but this had little impact on society at large. Furthermore, federal laws restricting public dissent soon curbed most citizens who opposed war. Those who persisted in their opposition to the war faced prosecution and prison terms or public attack with little legal recourse. And in more than a few instances it appeared that those accused of unpatriotic action were condemned without little, if any, real evidence. Regardless, the public sentiment against those who might try to voice their opinions was soon placed on notice. Less than a month after declaring war on Germany, the *Beaufort Gazette* warned its readers that if anyone had a German accent they better speak in whispers. The patriotism (or hysteria) generated by the new war status of the nation led the *Charleston News and Courier* to proclaim that in wartime the U.S. Constitution was less relevant compared to the nation's need for security and vigilance against its enemies. Perhaps one of the more extreme public refrains during this period came from the *Saluda Standard*, which advocated that those who opposed the government's war policy should be lynched.[41]

Even so there were some citizens of the state who continued to oppose the war, at least in the minds of some "patriotic" residents. And when this happened, retribution from local citizens could be severe. Federal officials arrested Carl Karst, a Charleston grocer and German immigrant, soon after Congress voted for war because someone had accused the grocer of threatening President Wilson's life. The outcome of this arrest is unknown, yet it seems that even if the grocer had made such a threat the means of implementing it were slim to none. Nonetheless, patriotic fervor led citizens and authorities alike to react with little or no reason. In another case an individual refused to purchase Liberty Bonds. In June 1918, a Chester candy proprietor was paraded by citizens of the town into the public square and, somewhat ironically under the Confederate Monument, forced to kiss the American flag three times. After that his erstwhile neighbors watched him sign a check for twenty-five dollars to the Red Cross fund.[42]

Such "patriotic" fervor by South Carolinians was fostered by state government and its governor in particular. Richard I. Manning already had declared that South Carolina should be the most patriotic state in the war effort. He backed his rhetoric with an aggressive program of loyalty oaths that he directed the State Council of Defense to administer. This included three campaigns against those who were termed slackers, citizens who either refused to do their part for the war effort or would not support the war effort through contributions to Liberty Loan Drives and war stamps. To back up the governor's words and codify what the State Council and the citizens of the state should do to support the war, a booklet entitled *The South Carolina Handbook of the War* was published in September 1917. Full of advice and warnings against "disloyal" actions, it began with a rationale for why the nation went to war and then had sections such as "Concerning Loyalty (No Room for Treachery and Rules for Disloyalists)" and another section on "How You Can Help Win the War," which listed such items as "Stop Criticizing; Cheer Up and Get Busy; One Hundred Per Cent Loyalty, and Subscribe to the Liberty Loan." It concluded with this dire warning: if the Germans were able to land on South Carolina's shores, they would "turn this land into a condition which would make General Sherman, if he were alive, apologize to Hell for speaking of war as hell."

In a final act of "extreme patriotic" fervor, in October 1917 Governor Manning delivered a speech before a Philadelphia audience. One of the nation's most vocal critics of the war was Wisconsin Senator Robert La Follette. He had been one of six in the Senate to vote against war, and he continued to oppose it through the summer. By the fall some Senate colleagues and several national newspapers were demanding that the Wisconsin legislator be sanctioned and expelled from the chamber. A few politicians and newspaper editors even demanded that La Follette should be tried and convicted of treason for his opposition. The South Carolina governor took up this demand in his speech but went further. He argued that such "treasonous" actions should not only result in La Follette's conviction but also his execution. But if the trial was unable to find enough evidence to sentence him to death then Manning wanted the senator to be deported. Fortunately for La Follette he was neither expelled nor tried. After the war, his opposition took on a more positive light among many of those who had condemned him during the war.[43]

The South Carolina Council of Defense was an extension of the federal Committee of Public Information that President Wilson established to galvanize public support for the war effort. Governor Manning fully supported the national effort and delegated the state council to follow the directive of the federal war agency. In line with this, Manning proclaimed early in the war that "if there is one spot in the United States where doubt, criticism and disloyalty should at present be unthinkable, that spot is South Carolina."[44] The council had committees organized in each of the state's forty-six counties and more than two thousand South Carolinians participated in projects ranging from

Governor Richard I. Manning (1859–1931)

Here the governor sits on a horse in front of his home in Columbia with a five-star service flag behind, 1918. He, like thousands of other Americans, had five sons serving in the war effort. A Sumter native, Manning was one of the few progressives in state politics who began his political career as a representative of his home district in 1892. Although part of the conservative wing who opposed Governor Tillman's policies then, Manning would become a supporter of many progressive policies on the national level, including better child labor laws, compulsory education for all children and economic development. When elected to his first term as governor in 1914 he quickly supported Wilson's policies, especially his plans to rebuild the U.S. armed forces in 1916. While leading the state into the war, he also made personal sacrifices. One of his sons was killed in the trenches in France near the war's conclusion.

trestle guards to anti-prostitution crusades. An important part of these smaller councils was also to recruit four thousand individuals, statewide, to promote the national war effort. These recruits were known as Four Minute Men because they gave four-minute presentations to groups of all sizes in theaters, churches and schools promoting patriotic support for war.

Yet as the nation geared up and recruitment of young men into the armed forces accelerated by the fall of 1917, many problems abounded. These ranged from housing shortages and transportation problems to a growing concern over the spread of venereal disease among soldiers and sailors stationed in camps around the state.

Some hardships were temporary in nature and arose due to severe weather conditions. The severe winter of 1917–18 was a period in which South Carolina communities had to make temporary sacrifices for heating and gas consumption. Thus in Greenville manufacturing plants closed down for five days in January and then ten Mondays thereafter to conserve coal reserves, often referred to as "Heatless Days." In many towns and cities businesses either closed on Mondays or, if they were opened for business that day, they were supposed to shut off the heat anyway. Likewise, Sunday driving was curtailed to save on gas consumption.[45]

This measure, however, was still temporary. For those communities that became hosts to new or revitalized military installations, the massive housing shortages caused by the influx of soldiers, sailors and their families remained through most of the war. Spartanburg might have had one of the worst problems in this regard because of its small population prior to the war. Estimated at twenty-six thousand before 1917, it doubled when the Twenty-seventh Division arrived in fall 1917, along with many family members in tow who wanted to remain near their fathers and husbands. Naturally friction arose in the community as every available home and apartment quickly was rented or leased within a few weeks by families who had moved south from New York. A few who had plenty of money even tried to purchase homes from the locals. One story people of the area remembered long after the war indicated the extremes to which some newcomers went to find accommodation. The mother of one New York soldier was determined to be as near to him as she could. So she found a house not far from the camp, went up to the door and asked the donor if she could rent his home. At first he and his family were reluctant but when she kept raising the offer, from $500 a month to $1,000 a month, the owner relented and moved into a nearby tenant house. But to their chagrin the new resident then proceeded to remodel their home to suit the sophisticated New Yorker's taste. When her son's division left for France in spring 1918, she returned the home to its owner and went back to New York. But while these stories may be somewhat apocryphal, the new money and prosperity the influx of new soldiers brought was not. Spartanburg businessmen saw their profit margins increase far beyond any they had experienced in years. In Charleston, housing shortages led navy authorities to appeal for residents to make any rooms they had available to outside workers. Efforts to build new housing for the influx of war workers was hampered by building supply shortages, and before most of the new construction really began, the war ended so that few were ever built.[46]

Although highways in the state did not exist in 1917, most of the state's larger communities had trolley systems that had been created by the 1890s. Cars were still in their infancy so most people depended on trolleys, bicycles or their two feet to get from place to place without much difficulty, except for in Charleston. There, where the navy yard was located several miles north of the city center, workers were dependent on trolleys. This quickly became a problem as the workforce expanded several fold in the first months of the war. By the end of 1917 navy yard employees complained that the Consolidated Company operating the trolley system provided inadequate service and that, despite many appeals to improve it over several months, it had still not taken action. In December the workers threatened to send a delegation to Washington, D.C., if improvement was not made by the new year. Apparently the problem persisted through the rest of the war. Even after the armistice was signed workers were upset with the transportation. In early 1919 a large demonstration through the center of Charleston was held by thousands of navy yard workers demanding that something be done about the "poor trolley car service." The demonstrators were accompanied by a naval band and all carried hundreds of protest signs.[47]

But these problems were minor, at least in the minds of some authorities, compared to the ever-present problem posed by prostitution. It seemed that every military installation, from the Upstate to the coast, had this illicit industry plaguing it; U.S. Army and Naval authorities wanted it eradicated before it harmed the new troops they were preparing for war. In Columbia military authorities took little time in meeting with city fathers to have an ordinance passed to outlaw the practice. In July city council met to consider the proposed law but also received a petition from five hundred businessmen with "restrictions," since they argued that to outlaw the illicit trade in the past had always failed. However, army authorities would not relent, even threatening to abandon the new camp before its completion. So the ordinance passed. By the end of the month police met with 99 women who lived in "recognized" houses to advise them that they must end their activities by August 1. To reinforce this decree churchwomen tried to assist by offering help to 115 prostitutes if they agreed to reform.[48] Interestingly, only 2 accepted. The others presumably left town or claimed they would set up boardinghouses. In spite of every effort by city authorities to end the practice, prostitution persisted, although in a less obvious fashion.

Similar efforts were made by naval authorities in Charleston to end prostitution in that city as the navy yard expanded, and the results were just as problematic. While an ordinance outlawed the practice, the trade could not be eliminated no matter what the authorities tried. In 1917, under the authority of Mayor Tristan T. Hyde, the Charleston police arrested fifty-four ladies and closed down the eight brothels near the central business district. However, instead of ending the trade, the ladies moved into a "respectable residential" area. And it appeared that even the respectable citizens of the city were not enthusiastic about the new laws, especially after Mayor Hyde ruthlessly attempted to impose the law, sometimes without due process. Some residents even protested that if the military insisted on such a policy they would not mind if the entire navy personnel left the area. But while the war lasted, the restrictive law remained in effect, even though vice was not eradicated. Soon after the armistice the restrictions on prostitution relaxed and the "oldest profession" returned to its former notoriety.[49]

As military authorities strove to persuade local and state authorities to eradicate prostitution, the South Carolina State Board of Health wrestled with other persistent diseases that had plagued the state for generations. These included tuberculosis, pellagra and malaria. By 1915 the state had finally provided funds to build and equip a small sanitarium north of Columbia for white tubercular patients (black patients would have to wait until after the war to have their own facility). Pellagra, a vitamin deficiency disease, had mystified medical science until the early 1900s, when research showed that its cure lay in improving diets with regular amounts of vitamins and minerals. By World War I the death rate from this had been significantly reduced, even though 497 deaths had occurred in 1918, a slight improvement from the year before, when the death rate had reached 544.[50]

War and thousands of recruits from around the country who came to South Carolina for training at one of the army or navy installations brought in a new scourge—cerebral-spinal meningitis. First appearing in December 1917 at Camp Jackson, it spread to the population in communities along the railway lines through which recruits came and, unknowingly, passed it on to civilians. By the end of 1918 state health officials claimed that 171 South Carolinians had died from it, a huge increase from the previous year, when 33 residents died.[51]

Such diseases, coupled with sexually transmitted ones, caused problems for the poorly staffed, under-funded State Board of Health, but these problems paled in comparison to the influenza epidemic that hit South Carolina in fall 1918. For a time political and health authorities seemed powerless to stem it. While it is uncertain how the flu started, one theory is that it originated at Camp Funston, an army training facility in Kansas where animals and recruits were in cramped conditions, allowing the virus to incubate and spread to the recruits, some of whom took it with them around the nation and over to Europe and the trenches. The first cases in South Carolina were reported in September. Charleston's Ladies Benevolent Society, which looked after the city's indigent families, reported their first case at the end of that month. Camp Jackson acknowledged the Midlands' first cases in the same month and by October the Columbia installation was off-limits to all outsiders. Meanwhile the citizens of the capital were soon plagued by so much illness that schools, theaters and the university were shut down and all public gatherings (except Liberty Bond rallies) were prohibited. A similar slowdown happened in other major towns around the state, including Greenville, Spartanburg and Florence.[52]

Although the epidemic did not effect the Southeast as badly as it did the Northeast, especially large cities such as New York, Boston and Philadelphia, it seemed to most in South Carolina to be just as bad. Yet until late September state news accounts of the disease remained vague and focused on its impact outside South Carolina. Like the national press, state and local presses minimized the coverage to prevent hysteria from gripping the population about the spread of the flu. It is hard to say if this helped in South Carolina. John Barry has argued in his recent study of the epidemic that in those communities that were hit the hardest in the Northeast, the lack of publicity and misinformation generated by the media seemed only to add to the citizens' anxiety and fear. And while such anxieties must have gripped South Carolina communities in the same period, much of what the local media reported focused on the problems outside the state until late September, when media coverage in the state on the flu became more comprehensive.[53]

As the flu ravaged Boston and Philadelphia, the *State* reported on September 17 that most of the flu was concentrated on naval bases. Yet a day later the same newspaper reported that cases in the state had dropped from previous reports, although it listed a few deaths in Columbia and around the state, including a child, and mentioned that some schools had been shut down. Influenza struck military installations in the state first, with Camp Jackson reporting its first cases on September 7 while it struck national guard camps in the Upstate nearly a month after. Not long after the first cases were reported, each military camp was quarantined in an effort to forestall the spread of the disease. The same issues faced the Charleston Navy Yard. Quarantined by the middle of September, one sailor recalled that "flu was raging through the camp like a pack of rabid wolves: men were dying every day." This sailor, the famous artist Norman Rockwell, came down with the virus and claimed that his life was saved because a doctor recognized him as he tried admitting himself into the base hospital. The physician, in no uncertain terms, warned him to get out immediately because the "germs are as thick as blackstrap molasses" in the infirmary. Instead Rockwell went back to his hammock, piled blankets on top of himself and sweat it out. Many civilians probably did similar things, especially if their entire family came down with the disease, since there was a tremendous shortage of nurses and doctors to attend to the sick throughout the state. At the height of the disease in late September and October, this problem grew more acute because so many healthcare workers fell ill as well.[54]

In an effort to prevent the disease from spreading, public announcements in newspapers and pamphlets told people not to gather in groups of any sort, to wear cloth facemasks over their noses and mouths whenever they were outside and keep homes and barracks ventilated so the germs could be dispersed. In military installations most officers ordered their soldiers to remain at least three feet apart when in formation. Bunks in the barracks were supposed to be spread out. At Camp Wadsworth the barracks actually were tents with wooden flooring. Normally eight men were housed in a tent, which resulted in very close quarters. As the flu began to threaten the Spartanburg camp, former Lieutenant E. Vaughn Gordy of the New York Twenty-seventh Division recalled years later that soldiers were ordered to place their cots outdoors in the company streets with at least ten feet between each. But, like the officers of Wadsworth and other installations in South Carolina and around the nation, people in the cities and towns discovered such measures as these did not prevent the virus from spreading. Each morning, when Gordy and fellow officers went out for morning inspections, there were always some who had to be taken to the hospital stricken with the flu. Occasionally some soldiers were found to have died overnight from the disease.[55]

During the worst period of the influenza epidemic in October, the *State*, which began to report more details about influenza in South Carolina, stated that Camp Jackson had 2,317 cases of influenza and 109 for pneumonia, with 13 deaths from the latter. In Greenville, Camp Sevier had 690 cases of influenza and 11 of pneumonia, with 3 deaths from the latter. Up the road in Camp Wadsworth only 2 cases of pneumonia had resulted in 1 death.[56] But this last appeared to mask the reality in Spartanburg. Susan Thoms's research shows that Camp Wadsworth was quarantined "against the city" and that by middle October local death reports showed 61 soldiers and 1 female nurse had died. One physician who cared for the sick claimed after the war that the base hospital report listed 600 cases of flu on October 14 with 9 deaths the previous day. The death toll for the entire month at Wadsworth put the numbers who succumbed to the epidemic at 57 whites and 22 black soldiers. Because it is difficult to be certain, the highest death rate at the camp during fall 1918 resulted in 178 deaths. This made up nearly 44 percent of the total deaths in the camp during its short existence (the total who died was 409). So it appeared that influenza, or complications from it, caused just under half the deaths at Wadsworth. During the same period, 510 Spartanburg citizens died of the flu.[57]

As in most of the country, by early October South Carolina towns and cities belatedly tried to prevent the disease from spreading by closing down most public places, from movie theaters and libraries to church services and parks. For the most part communities kept these in place until days before the armistice was announced a month later. On September 21 the paper printed advice from the Camp Jackson surgeon on what to do to prevent the spread of the flu. He advised, "Don't spit, wash hands regularly, avoid dust, keep floors clean, and turn one's head at least six feet away from other people before coughing." Although today we know these really don't help prevent the disease from spreading, this was the best that medical science could recommend in 1918 since nothing like it had ever struck with so much devastation before.[58]

Of the few personal accounts of the flu, John Huntley of Rock Hill gives a brief but revealing glimpse into how this disease affected individual families. On September 28 he wrote in his diary that Spanish influenza was becoming an epidemic in the nation while two acquaintances in town had come down with it. By early October he observed that the flu was spreading in his city. Without any comments he reported on October 5 that a government car "with relics" and Liberty Bond speakers were in town that evening for two hours, to which thousands of people came to listen. Then he reported that Elizabeth, his daughter, had come down with the disease the previous evening. Fortunately, she began to improve a few days later, but in the meantime there were "hundreds of cases in Rock Hill and many deaths." One family he knew had lost five of eight children and another couple had both died. By October 14 he claimed the flu was "raging here." And as he focused on the surrender of Germany and its allies in early November, he reported two months later that the flu was back with his wife stricken and many others in "Town and Country" also affected.[59]

Huntley's personal observations about the flu's persistence after 1918 were confirmed by the State Board of Health. Among various counties from Greenville in the west to the Pee Dee Counties in the east, fear of the disease remained high. In the north-central rural county of Chesterfield several prominent businessmen and the county's local member of the council of defense petitioned the governor to stop the local Chesterfield County Fair, scheduled for late November. With several cases of flu reported in communities from Cheraw in the east to Pageland in the west, the petitioners appealed to state officials "for humanitarians sake...at once" to stop the fair from happening. In spite of this desperate appeal the county fair took place anyway at the end of November. Yet as the new year began, the State Board of Health advised the governor that the flu remained a major problem and that without further financial aid and more staff they feared that many more flu-related deaths would occur.[60]

In the end the total number of cases were only rough estimates for the state and the nation. One historian estimated that between 150,000 and 400,000 South Carolina residents came down with the disease and between 4,000 and 10,000 died. By comparison the losses for the nation were more staggering. In John Barry's chilling story of the national epidemic, he estimated the total number of deaths at nearly 675,000, almost nine times the number of Americans killed on the Western Front. The impact on those children orphaned when their parents died is difficult to fathom, while many others who survived the disease often faced difficult complications that we can only vaguely comprehend.[61]

Even though the disease would continue into the new year and had further impact on the nation and state, the worst period of the epidemic had seemingly dissipated by November 1918. By now most people focused attention on celebrations once the armistice was signed ending the conflict. But while everyone greeted the news of Germany's capitulation with joy, most also must have been relieved by the decline of the flu that had affected everyone in some way. As the guns on the Western Front fell silent on the eleventh hour of the eleventh day in Europe, the information quickly reached towns in South Carolina. Although the news initially reached most people in the state early on the morning of November 11, most communities did not begin to celebrate in earnest until near noon of the same day. At midday in Greenville "every device was brought into use to make a noise."[62] Mills closed by that time, as did many stores, so that employees could join in the celebrations. By nightfall thousands thronged the streets "ringing bells, waving flags, shooting fireworks and throwing talcum powder" (since the stock of confetti in the city had been exhausted). Adding to the festive occasion were thousands of soldiers from Camp Sevier who were allowed to join in the revelry.[63]

Similar kinds of joy burst out in communities of all sizes. On the coast the residents of little Beaufort had a parade where the marine corps band came to enliven the festivities. Church services of thanksgiving took place and fireworks and church bells added to everyone's happiness. To sum up the mood at the end of the day, an aged Gullah woman remarked in a traditional fashion, "Do Jesus tank Gawd, I feel so light."[64]

With war over, South Carolinians hoped for the prosperity that the conflict had brought to continue. Unfortunately the euphoria of victory would soon turn to economic depression and disillusionment. The coming economic depression began in some parts of the state even before the end of the war, when the boll weevil reached the southern portions of the state and devastated the cotton crops in Beaufort County and other

The Flu Epidemic

It is estimated that 650,000 Americans died from this disease, most in a matter of a few short months in the fall of 1918. Although scientists are still arguing over its origins, one theory is that Camp Funston in Kansas, near Fort Riley, was the source. There, in February 1918, a large cattle herd was kept near a huge training center with thousands of men in close quarters, and the virus spread from animals to humans. Initially the disease caused only mild symptoms but with time the virus grew stronger (and lethal) and spread, as troops moved across country and then overseas, carrying the virus with them. Its first outbreak was noticed at Camp Devon, outside Boston, in August 1918. It quickly spread from there into the city and then south to Philadelphia and New York and then west. The first reports in South Carolina came in September, first appearing at the Charleston Navy Yard and then Camp Jackson. By October the flu had infected the populations of most towns and cities to the point that community leaders imposed curfews and shut down most public places, including church services and schools. Although the infection seemed to subside enough to lift the ban on public meetings in November, just days before the armistice was declared, smaller outbreaks continued into 1919. It is estimated that 4,000 to 10,000 South Carolinians died from the disease and its complications while about 200,000 became sick but recovered.

What were the symptoms?
Most people who contracted the flu first complained of headaches that grew severe along with a high fever. Often this would turn into pneumonia and the patient began coughing up dark mucus while their face and extremities turned blue from oxygen deficiency. Generally the disease struck young adults more than other age groups and caused the greatest mortality rates in this age bracket. Some scientists argue that this group had the least immunity to the flu and thus could not fight off the virus as well as those who were older and had been exposed to it at an earlier age. It was not uncommon for people to show symptoms in the morning and die within twenty-four to forty-eight hours.

nearby areas by December 1917. First reported on Daufuskie Island in early November 1917, the insect consumed 70 percent of the crop there before the end of the year. Twelve months later the pest had reached beyond the Broad River to Port Royal, Lady's and St. Helena Islands and then penetrated up the Savannah River into Allendale and Barnwell Counties. Even as the boll weevil took its toll of cotton production, what was

Some of the nurses at the main hospital, Camp Sevier. These dedicated women nursed many soldiers back from injury and illness. They were especially crucial during the flu epidemic that struck all the camps throughout the state in fall 1918. *Courtesy South Carolina Room, Greenville County Public Library.*

harvested brought less and less to its growers. At first prices remained high and up through the first half of 1921 cotton sold for 40 cents a pound. However, by the end of the year, it sold for less than half that, 13.5 cents a pound, and with it most farmers' prosperity quickly came to an end.[65]

Such a catastrophe, coupled with the slowdown in exports as the European economies began to recover, eventually saw the rest of the state's farming economy go into a tailspin of depression that it did not recover from until Pearl Harbor, two decades later. Other aspects of the economy did not fare much better. Spurred on by demobilization of all the military installations in the state, employment for many residents declined rapidly and prospects became bleak for any improvement. Camps Sevier and Wadsworth closed their operations by spring 1919, and within another two years Camp Jackson was demobilized. Virtually all the thousands of buildings constructed on these installations in such haste early in the war were quickly offered for sale and dismantled, while the rest were simply destroyed by wrecking crews. The lands leased for the camps were returned to their original owners or to public entities for educational, recreational and industrial use. Consequently, portions of Camp Jackson became sites for a Boy Scout and Girl Scout camp and the YMCA maintained a summer camp. On the other hand, the golf course established by the army remained in use and continued to be a popular place for avid golfers through the interwar years. Although the U.S. Army officially abandoned the site in April 1922, portions of it were reclaimed three years later for use by the South Carolina National Guard as a summer encampment. Nonetheless, most local businesses near the camps suffered now that thousands of recruits no longer trained nearby.[66]

On the coast the navy's installations survived, but barely. Although the U.S. Navy tried to close the navy yard in Charleston in the early twenties, an extensive lobbying effort by the state's Congressional delegation prevented this. Nonetheless its operation barely continued. The huge reduction in its labor force from nearly ten thousand at the peak of the war to less than a twentieth of this by the mid-1920s was due, in part, to a general demobilization by the U.S. armed forces. Naval expansion, curtailed by the 1922 International Washington Naval Conference, saw the five main naval powers in the world agree to limit and reduce naval armaments and ship tonnage to a specified level. The U.S. Navy reduced its main battleship fleet and lesser-sized war vessels while curtailing ship construction significantly until the late 1930s. Consequently the duties of the yard were restricted to occasional ship refitting and it would not build another warship until the mid-1930s. The marine depot on Parris Island remained active but at a reduced level until the end of the same decade.[67]

Amidst demobilization and the sudden collapse of farm prices, South Carolinians had a few long-lasting benefits to derive from their patriotic service during the war. While the conflict had lifted its isolation from the rest of the nation by bringing thousands of people, both military and nonmilitary, into the state, it also had given some natives the chance to see life outside the Palmetto State. Whether training at a military camp outside South Carolina or going overseas to fight the "Hun," it gave many from the state a new perspective on life and a different approach to living when soldiers came home. The influx of newcomers, even though brief, provided prosperity to many local businesses and, perhaps more importantly, gave many natives a chance to interact with other Americans for the first time. This fostered some new, long-lasting relationships. In more than a few cases soldiers from New York, California and elsewhere met local women, married and settled down in their adopted state after the war. In Spartanburg, New York native E. Vaughn Gordy trained at Camp Wadsworth, where he met his future bride and Upstate native, Beulah Gentry. After the war he returned to Spartanburg, married Beulah and settled down to raise a family and start a business.[68]

In Charleston another outsider met a local girl, married and remained to raise a family. Ora Cecil "John" Johnston, a native of northern California, found his way to the South Carolina coast. A sailor in the U.S. Navy's submarine fleet, Johnston met the young Charlestonian Gertrude Marie Pieper while on leave. With the armistice, it was not long before he mustered out of the navy and proposed to the young Miss Pieper, whose family had lived in the city for generations. Although his proposal was accepted, his bride-to-be made it clear she would not leave her family home. Johnston accepted the conditions. After their marriage the native of California became an adopted son of the community, raising a family and almost reaching the age of one hundred before he passed away.[69]

As for women of the state, their most tangible achievement that emerged from the war was the Nineteenth Amendment, which gave them the right to vote. Although women had been striving to get the vote prior to the Civil War, the changing roles of women that World War I initiated provided most Americans with the last proof needed that the female gender's political rights could no longer be ignored. Even so South Carolina's legislature was one of the few in the nation not to accept the new amendment; its conservative stance was negated by a two-thirds majority of the nation's other state legislatures, which ratified it in 1920. Just two months after this ratification South Carolina women voted in national and state elections for the first time.[70]

As for African Americans, their opportunities garnered by the war effort were largely abrogated in the postwar period. The Charleston race riot of May 1919 showed the fragile condition of race relations in the aftermath of the armistice. When white sailors and local blacks got into a fight on one of the city's main streets, it precipitated a night of violence in large portions of downtown, particularly on King and Meeting Streets. Aided by local whites, military and naval personnel raided two shooting galleries, beat up blacks they found and destroyed a black-owned barbershop called Fridie's. Local police, with the assistance of another marine detachment, were able to quell the riot by morning the next day. Before it was over two blacks were dead and seventeen others wounded, including a thirteen-year-old boy who was paralyzed from the hips down. Seven white sailors and one policeman were injured. Despite the climate of the time, a coroner's jury blamed the attacks on the sailors and marines. However, it appeared that little punishment resulted for those responsible.[71]

Such violence does not seem to have been duplicated in other South Carolina communities, but it left a pall on many in the state, particularly African Americans. This became another reason for many minorities to leave Charleston and the state for new opportunities in Northeastern and Midwestern industrial centers, where better jobs and the prospects of a better life were opened to them. The state's black population dropped from 55.2 percent in 1910 to 51.4 percent a decade later. Because of reduced numbers those blacks who remained had less competition for some postwar jobs, even though the wartime opportunities that had opened to blacks at military installations now disappeared. Black farmers who had seen their incomes improve during the war made some advances materially, which had led to the opening of four new black-owned banks during and after the war. And finally, some whites stepped forward to campaign for improved social and economic rights for African Americans so they would have a more equitable place in the society. While negative in his conclusion, even former governor Duncan Heyward stated that the state must accept the new reality of a "moving spirit of world democracy," since many South Carolina minorities who had served overseas were returning home with a determination for change backed by their military training in weapons. The only way to stem this was to promote white immigration in order to create a white majority in the state.[72]

On a local level, at least in Columbia and Charleston, small groups of whites endeavored to improve postwar race relations. The Columbia attorney Beverly Herbert, along with others such as businessman James H. Gibbes, tried a more positive approach in dealing with racial issues. They advocated improved legal status for African Americans and more equitable opportunities. Likewise in Charleston, a biracial committee made up of whites and blacks was organized to seek better opportunities for its minority population. Along with these basic goals, the two committees sought to improve other aspects of life for everyone, such as more paved highways, better law and order and better schools. Although these efforts had limited impact during the interwar period, they became a new push by some in the white community that would be revived in later decades with better results.[73]

And to give further hints of optimism to a postwar era, the state's most paternalistic organization, which had desperately tried for half a century to redefine the causes of the American Civil War and Reconstruction, seemed to rekindle their respect and patriotism for America in its time of need. Throughout the war the United Daughters of the Confederacy (UDC) had promoted patriotic work and support for the American soldier at home and abroad. This renewed interest in America crystallized in the early postwar era was signified in one rural county when the Edgefield chapter of the UDC observed during the first Memorial Day after the armistice,

> *Many changes have taken place during the past year but none was more marked than the attitude of the United Daughters of the Confederacy. We still honor and love our (Confederate) veterans and hold our sacred Memorial Day for them...but we have attained to a broader outlook, and many of us who once blindly worshipped the Stars and Bars can now look with pride and glory upon this other flag, this wondrous flag of freedom under which we sent our darling boys across the seas and which has come to mean even more than the worshipped Stars and Bars.*[74]

"A Wonderful War in Every Way":
Columbia during the Great War

Kristina K. Dunn, Historic Columbia Foundation, Inc.

I am not unaware of History and have been frequently chided for such a callous statement, but World War I became for Columbia a wonderful war in every way." When writing her memoirs in 1970, Margaret Green Devereux pinpointed the events of the Great War as a watershed moment for her life and the course of Columbia's history. Although looking back on her life with a strong sense of nostalgia, Devereux noted some key events that reflected life in Columbia during World War I. She noted the numerous Columbia men who served in the war and how few casualties there were out of those men. She also praised the homefront efforts of Columbians, such as housing English children, high-ranking officers and visiting families. For Devereux, the establishment of Camp Jackson brought the excitement of charming officers and soldiers enjoyed through the whirlwind of dances, concerts and plays. The result of this activity was a greater connectedness of Columbia with the outside world, bringing new people and opportunities.[1]

During the early spring of 1917, the United States anxiously waited and watched to see what President Woodrow Wilson would do about the changing events in Europe. Although not a native South Carolinian, Wilson had spent some of his teenage years in Columbia and still had familial and friendship connections to the city. The personal ties that Wilson held to Columbia heightened the tension for many of its citizens. On April 3, 1917, Columbians went to work as if it was any other day, but by mid-afternoon the city was abuzz with the latest *Columbia Record* headline: "United States is Really at War." Even though the headline was a few days premature of the actual declaration of war, the thick block-print letters emphasized the importance of these new developments. Then, on April 6, Congress authorized Wilson's pro-war stance and the United States was officially at war. Following their president's lead, Columbians prepared themselves for the upcoming patriotic trial.[2]

Spurred into action by the events in early April, Columbians went to work preparing the city for wartime work. Columbians established a canteen corps in order to assist the soldiers passing through Columbia on trains. Additionally, Dr. James A Haynes organized a local Red Cross chapter on April 4. The following day a "patriotic demonstration" was held to celebrate the Red Cross as well as to reaffirm the patriotism and preparedness of Columbians. The Red Cross Preparation Day Parade began at Elmwood and Main Streets, ending with a rally at the statehouse grounds. Participants included soldiers, "Uncle Sam," the Boy Scouts, the Campfire Girls, the Wade Hampton Chapter of the United Confederate Veterans, the United Daughters of the Confederacy, the Girls of the '60s (a social club whose members had lived through the Civil War) and other community participants. The chairman of the preparedness day celebration, Joe Sparks, commented, "Now is the time for Columbians to let it be known in no uncertain terms that they stand squarely behind the nation and President Wilson in this emergency." Overall, this parade demonstrated local patriotism and homefront preparedness instead of military might.[3]

Along with homefront preparedness efforts, the city and state initiated groundwork for the development of the state's military readiness. The Columbia YMCA held their first military training class in Columbia on April 4. Additionally, Governor Richard Manning pronounced Wednesday, April 11, as Naval Recruiting Day and established quotas for all South Carolina counties. Lexington County's recruiting goal was eighteen men and Richland County had a quota of twenty-nine men. These types of recruiting goals continued throughout the war. However, local businessmen were in charge of a project that would have the greatest impact on the economic and population development of the city.[4]

Private businessmen had been soliciting the federal government to establish an army fort, or cantonment site, in the Columbia area for several years prior to the war. During March of 1912, their efforts were rewarded when the federal government declared Columbia to be the mobilization center of South Carolina if a military emergency should arise. When diplomatic relations with Germany continued to decline, local business leader Edwin Robertson used this federal declaration to lobby Washington for a military camp. In January of 1917, army officials visited a site east of the city in order to study the feasibility of the area for a camp. Confident of the success of his plan, Robertson and other business leaders met in the Manson Building (which later housed the Berry's on Main department store) on the corner of Main and Taylor Streets with the Greater Columbia Chamber of Commerce's Cantonment Committee to raise money to acquire options on real estate in the area. The plan worked and on May 19, 1917, General Douglas MacArthur officially announced that Columbia would become one of sixteen national cantonment sites.[5]

The new cantonment site, called Camp Jackson (later Fort Jackson), provided jobs to men in the community and boosted patronage of local businesses. By August 26, 1917, the camp employed 9,592 men at an average salary of $3.34 per day for white workers. Blacks, on the other hand, received only about $1.75 per day. These salaries were in addition to free housing, which was segregated. In order to encourage these workers and future soldiers to patronize local businesses, the Columbia City Trolley Company had a new line operating to Camp Jackson by mid-August. This trolley line served the dual purpose of connecting Camp Jackson with Columbia's resources while allowing Columbians to take advantage of the new business opportunities and social life developments, such as dances and theater outings.[6]

Rapid population growth of incoming soldiers and personnel along with the development of buildings soon made Camp Jackson a city within a city. On September 5, 1917, the first white draftees arrived at the camp. The first black draftees arrived the following month. The camp housed elements of the Thirtieth Division before getting ordered to Camp Sevier. The Eighty-first Wildcat Division and the Fifth Division were organized and trained in the Midlands during the war. By July 1918, the population of the camp peaked at 44,242 men. Camp Jackson boasted soldier housing, mess halls, a theater, officers' quarters, a library, training fields, a hospital and other buildings totaling around $12 million worth of construction. In spite of these facilities, the personnel stationed at the camp continued to interact with Columbia-area citizens and businesses, helping to create a boom in the local economy.[7]

Local businesses placed advertisements directed at soldiers and officers in the Columbia Record and the Torch and Camp, which was a publication sponsored by the State newspaper and the YMCA specifically for soldiers at Camp Jackson. Officer dress shoes, clothing, lunch specials, theatrical plays and musical performances were targeted at those stationed at Camp Jackson. Advertisements were also directed to those doing any type of war work, such as Doan's Kidney Pills. Their advertisement declared, "Can't 'Do Your Bit' With a Bad Back" and featured a worker making munitions, thus seizing on current wartime propaganda to help sell their product.[8]

In order to demonstrate their support of the American soldiers, Columbians participated in a myriad of patriotic activities, such as book drives to gather reading material for soldiers. Specific requests for children's books were widespread in order to help solve low literacy rates at Camp Jackson. The Columbia Chapter of the Red Cross also sponsored campaigns to ease the burden of soldiers. For example, on April 14, 1918, the Red Cross sold chewing gum from a booth downtown. Columbians could opt to purchase the chewing gum for the soldiers fighting in France, or purchase the gum for their own use and have the proceeds go to support military causes. Local relief societies also purchased a building on the corner of Main and Taylor Streets for the soldiers' recreation, including activities such as dancing, reading and games.[9] Additionally, Columbians participated in raising money to support the national war machine.

Columbians participated in the nationwide Liberty Loan Drives that encouraged citizens to buy bonds that would assist in financially supporting the federal government during the war. The local newspapers ran advertisements to notify the public about the campaigns. Additionally, local campaign workers organized parades to remind civilians of their patriotic duty to support the Liberty Loan Drives. As Margaret Devereux noted in her memoirs, the parades "kept us wild with pride and patriotic fever." Although similar to the nationalistic spirit of the April 1917 Red Cross Preparation Day Parade, the Liberty Loan parades concentrated more on military power and winning the war than a general community exhibition.[10]

The Second Liberty Loan Parade in Columbia occurred at noon on Wednesday, October 3, 1917. Starting at the statehouse, the parade progressed up Main Street and ended at Laurel Street. Soldiers and officers from Camp Jackson participated in the festivities in attempts to embolden Columbians with the army's grand demonstration of tanks, rifles and servicemen. In addition to selling bonds, the Second Liberty Loan Campaign focused on daily efforts that could make a difference during the war. On the day following the parade, the women of Columbia were invited to a discussion about food conservation and the establishment of Victory Gardens. The women of Columbia were also encouraged to save kitchen waste, such as fruit pits and nutshells, which could be used in the manufacture of gas masks. In order to further this effort, Governor Manning declared November 9, 1918, Gas Mask Day to help encourage the collection of these materials for the production of gas masks for soldiers in France.[11]

Columbia held the Fourth Liberty Loan Parade on Saturday, September 28, 1918. At noon, five planes flew overhead and dropped Liberty Loan flyers, signaling the beginning of the parade. Approximately fifteen thousand soldiers accompanied by artillery pieces proceeded down Main Street for about two hours under a steady rain. The Columbia Chapter of the American Red Cross helped by escorting convalescent soldiers from Camp Jackson to Elmwood Avenue to watch the parade and women from the neighborhood brought apples as a special treat for the recovering men. This last Liberty Loan campaign during the fall of 1918 continued many of the same patriotic traditions of the previous Liberty Loan Drives. However, there was a notable difference in how Columbia handled issues of race during the campaign.[12]

War Garden at 615 Pickens Street. *Courtesy Historic Columbia Foundation.*

The Fourth Liberty Loan Drive signaled a new course in race relations for the war effort in Columbia. In order to help with the bond drive, the white community began to actively recruit African American participation in the selling process. On September 29, 1918, African American Liberty Loan workers were sworn into service in order to help sell bonds specifically to the African American community. Prior to this campaign, African American involvement was expected and praised, but not actively nurtured. Even this announcement came with a degree of distrust by the white community due to stereotypes of African American laziness and inferiority. White Columbians worried that African American workers would not work wholeheartedly toward collecting money and that members of the African American community were not patriotic enough for the American cause to give any significant amount of money. The *Columbia Record* published statements by Reverend J.C. White, who was in charge of the Fourth Liberty Loan Drive in the African American community. He warned the African American participants to follow the rules and to have a high work ethic:

> *The workers that have been assigned must work unceasingly or they must step aside not feign "loyalty" and "patriotism" without exemplifying it and hope to share equally in the free advertisement and glory gained by those who do the real work...But the laws of public sentiment are convicting you each day, and it is proposed by the committee to keep an exacting record of all workers who will do their full share, that they may have due credit there for.*

African American women watching the Fourth Liberty Loan Parade as it passes by the Columbia Hospital on a rainy September 28, 1918. *Courtesy Historic Columbia Foundation.*

Reverend White feared that any accusations of individuals not working to their fullest would bolster stereotypes of laziness and unpatriotic behavior of the black community and undermine their pursuit of equality in a Jim Crow society. He hoped that the Liberty Loan Drive would increase the positive image of African Americans in Columbia and lead to a new social respect for the postwar years.[13]

In spite of the positive economic and social impacts on the city, not all of Camp Jackson's influences were as welcome. Citizens worried about the influx of soldiers bringing disease. In order to alleviate some of these concerns, the government attempted to regulate the city's food markets and closed known places of prostitution. During late November of 1917, a meningitis outbreak at Camp Jackson had the citizens of Columbia advocating for a total quarantine of the camp. In spite of their best protests, the army did not support a total quarantine. However, the citizens' complaints highlight the larger issue of the spread of diseases such as meningitis, measles and pneumonia with the area population increase. During these epidemics, Columbia's Baptist Hospital began to treat the army patients if the Camp Jackson Hospital was filled beyond capacity.[14]

One of the worst disease outbreaks occurred during the fall of 1918, when Camp Jackson and Columbia fought the global Spanish influenza pandemic. Approximately five thousand soldiers and officers at Camp Jackson were treated for the illness, of which three hundred died. During the epidemic, the city of Columbia enforced a strict quarantine of public gathering spaces. For four weeks, Columbia's churches, schools, theaters and soda fountains were closed in order to stop the rapid spread of the disease. The influenza outbreak did not discriminate against its victims and many people of all races, classes and ages became deathly ill. The graves in local Columbia cemeteries tell the story of a disastrous October of 1918. Notable examples include Samuel Sweeny Koneman, who died at age ten, and Viola Shull Hite, who died at age thirty-seven, leaving behind a husband and a ten-year-old daughter. Both victims were buried in Columbia's Elmwood Cemetery. Twenty-one-year-old Citadel graduate Reginald V. Dicks died from influenza while attending officer training school at Camp Gordon in Georgia. His family erected a monument to him in Elmwood Cemetery that displays the image of a doughboy soldier charging the enemy. Although Dicks never engaged the enemy in battle, the monument emphasizes that he died while in service of his country, allowing the family to give a larger meaning to his life and death. This memorial suggests that his death was as significant as if he had been killed on the frontlines. The quarantine in Columbia was lifted on November 4, 1918. The *Columbia Record* described the excitement of returning to normal life, but with a hint of fatalism, writing that "were it not for the many newly made graves in the cemeteries of the city it might be possible to forget that the dreadful epidemic had ever visited us." Fittingly, the end of the quarantine and the abatement of the influenza outbreak's deadly tempest occurred while military tensions were also easing.[15]

When the warring countries finally declared a ceasefire to the hostilities, Columbians organized a celebration with the same vigor and enthusiasm as they had with the declaration of war. At 9:00 a.m. on November 11, 1918, bells and whistles rang out

The grave of Reginald V. Dicks, who died at Camp Gordon, Georgia, during the Spanish influenza outbreak. His family interred Dicks at Elmwood Cemetery in Columbia and placed this marker as a reminder of his desire to serve his country. *Courtesy Historic Columbia Foundation.*

on the streets of the city to celebrate Armistice Day. Columbia's mayor, R.J. Blalock, asked all Columbia businesses to close at 4:00 p.m. in order to engage in citywide celebrations. As the *Columbia Record* stated, "Columbia is this afternoon celebrating the end of the greatest war the world has ever known." With the celebrations, however, the editor of the *Columbia Record* pleaded with readers, "With the war won and the nation's army about to face the greatest task remaining in Europe, Columbia and South Carolina in common with the rest of the country, took up enthusiastically Monday morning the all-important business of seeing that the soldiers overseas have a continuation of the comforts and cheers afforded them" during the war. Accordingly, they continued to raise donations for the soldiers remaining overseas and those returning to Camp Jackson for discharge. Columbians also continued work on a Red Cross building at Camp Jackson in order to continue to see to the health and comfort of those soldiers still stationed there.[16] In spite of the serious nature of continuing

The band of the Thirtieth Division playing music to liven the crowd and celebrate the return of the soldiers on April 1, 1919, in Columbia. *Courtesy Historic Columbia Foundation.*

military-related work, the armistice signaled the advent of another round of parades and celebrations to support the troops returning to Camp Jackson.

On the first of April, Columbians celebrated the return of approximately 7,700 soldiers from the Thirtieth Division. The *Columbia Record* heralded, "Columbia is to celebrate as she never celebrated before the return of the men who broke the Hindenburg line and who have earned the record of being the finest fighters in the A.E.F." The parade started at 3:00 p.m. at the corner of Greene and Harden Streets. Five military bands accompanied the men of the Thirtieth Division while they paraded down Gervais Street and up Main Street. At the end of the parade, the troops were released to enjoy a large celebration that included dances, music and food. The Universities of South Carolina, Tennessee and North Carolina had booths at the festival in order to help reconnect friends and family in student and alumnae areas. Local businesses helped to sponsor the festivities. The Columbia Coca-Cola Bottling Company furnished four thousand free bottles of Coca-Cola for the soldiers and helped supply the rest of the festival.[17]

Four days later, Columbia celebrated the return of soldiers from the front lines with two more parades. The first parade was held during the morning of April 5 at Olympia Mill in order to celebrate the return of the 105th Ammunition Train. That afternoon, a larger celebration was held downtown to herald the arrival of the 119th Infantry back from Europe. The highlight of the afternoon parade was the addition of many of the 30th Division soldiers who had been recently discharged and participated in the day's activities as civilians.[18] In spite of the numerous parades that were now becoming almost routine in the city, Columbians continued to maintain their energy and excitement toward supporting the men returning from Europe.

Soldiers celebrating their return to Columbia by marching in a parade on April 1, 1919. *Courtesy Historic Columbia Foundation.*

Cavalry followed by the band of the Thirtieth Division down the streets of Columbia on April 1, 1919. *Courtesy Historic Columbia Foundation.*

Cavalry soldiers on the first of April 1919 parading down the street. *Courtesy Historic Columbia Foundation.*

Local businesses once again quickly seized upon a new business opportunity. In the local newspapers as well as the specific Camp Jackson newspaper, businesses placed "welcome back" advertisements. Car dealerships and home builders filled the newspapers with advertisements that thanked the soldiers for their service and encouraged soldiers to embrace new purchases to fulfill the postwar American dream. The Camp Jackson Studio placed advertisements reminding soldiers to have their photograph taken in their uniform before heading home. Area colleges placed announcements to promote new academic programs and employers solicited soldiers to stay in Columbia.[19]

One interesting advertisement was placed by former Governor Cole Blease: "While I opposed the boys going across, and future events will show who was right, yet I knew that they would do their duty and do it well and no one is prouder of their record than I, or happier to see them Home. God bless all of them."[20] Blease's advertisement highlights the fact that in spite of the patriotic calls for war, not all Columbians agreed with the war. For instance, around the beginning of the war on April 2, 1917, approximately two hundred citizens gathered at the Lexington County Courthouse to protest America's entry into the war. Now that the war was over, some of those citizens felt the need to reiterate their patriotism to the returning soldiers. Regardless of pre-war sentiments, Columbians banded together in 1919 to celebrate the returning soldiers.

Approximately 3,400 Richland County men and women served in the military during World War I. Of these individuals, there were 2,033 white soldiers and 1,350 blacks soldiers. Mortality rates were relatively low with only 62 whites and 40 blacks dying during their service time. However, this figure does not include the numerous soldiers

Tanks rolling down the streets of Columbia in April of 1919. *Courtesy Historic Columbia Foundation.*

Soldiers marching down the streets of Columbia on parade on April 1, 1919. *Courtesy Historic Columbia Foundation.*

Soldiers at ease before or after the parade on April 1, 1919. *Courtesy Historic Columbia Foundation.*

who had been injured or exposed to mustard gas, causing permanent damage. Caroline Girardeau, who was one of the original 5 enthusiasts of the Columbia Red Cross and the canteen corps, had 2 sons serving in the Great War. One of her sons, Charles Girardeau, enlisted at nineteen years old and served in the famous Forty-second Rainbow Division, which General MacArthur eventually led. The division saw action at the Battle of Champagne and around the Verdun front. Unfortunately, Charles Girardeau suffered from the effects of gas poisoning until his untimely death several years after the war's end. One of Columbia's Veterans of Foreign Wars posts is named in his honor. The surviving men and a handful of female army nurses and yeomanettes returned to Columbia with new ideas about life, death and social order.[21]

Most white servicemen returning from Europe to Columbia were filled with the hope of discovering new opportunities and reestablishing their civilian life. However, African American soldiers returned to Columbia uncertain of how they would be received and cautiously optimistic about improved race relations. White Americans feared that black servicemen had been exposed to ideas such as racial equality while in France and that they would demand those same rights and an end to Jim Crow laws when they returned home. The white community feared that the African American community would demand these rights through all means necessary. Thus, the summer of 1919 was filled with racial tension that many Columbians feared would spill over into violence. In order to ease the volatile tension, most black and white leaders advocated a return to the pre-war status quo. The effort succeeded and racial tensions eased with little change to the existing social structure. However, the African American community became largely disenchanted with their pacifist leaders and the constant need to bend to the idea of separate but equal. The old guard leadership no longer met the needs of many younger African Americans who wanted to demand their equal rights. Thus, stronger and louder voices that pushed for social change soon replaced the old guard leaders. Events in the African American community, including the ideas formulated by World War I and leadership changes, began a series of events that would eventually help to bring about major social reform in later years.[22]

In addition to social and economic changes, the war also changed Columbia's built environment. From the buildings of Camp Jackson to the new flourishing businesses and residences, Columbia's landscape was marked by the impact of the Great War. Columbians, however, desired to establish permanent monuments to the people who

Civilians supporting the soldiers of the Thirtieth Division as they pass by on parade. *Courtesy Historic Columbia Foundation.*

brought the country through the war, specifically to President Wilson and soldiers who served or died while enlisted.

The first initiative for a permanent memorial began in 1919 when Governor Manning proposed a World War Memorial Building to be located in Columbia. The South Carolina General Assembly approved the measure and appropriated $100,000 for its construction. Before construction could begin, however, the General Assembly had to re-appropriate the funds to combat the economic problems of the Great Depression. The War Memorial Commission redesigned the building to half of its original size and began a fundraising campaign, mainly through private subscriptions. The Public Works Administration granted the War Memorial Commission $33,200 in 1934, which allowed construction to begin on the building in 1935.[23]

On May 30, 1935, the cornerstone of the building was laid. The cornerstone contained a complete roster of all the men and women from South Carolina who served in World War I. Construction on the building was finished and a formal dedication exercise was held on March 23, 1937. Initially, the South Carolina Historical Commission located its offices inside the building, but the building was not sufficient for their needs and they relocated in 1947. The building's memorial-like design and interior chapel altar made it difficult to house any state agencies and it has housed numerous tenants since its completion.[24]

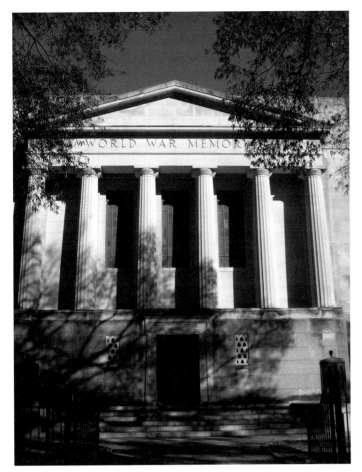

The World War Memorial Building, which was completed in 1937. Originally, the building was designed to hold the state archives and to serve as a memorial chapel. After serving a myriad of functions, currently the University of South Carolina utilizes the building for office space. *Courtesy Historic Columbia Foundation.*

In addition to the War Memorial Building, South Carolinians established other monuments to remember their ties to the Great War, such as the preservation of the Woodrow Wilson family home. The Wilson home on Hampton Street had undergone two different owners after the Wilson family left Columbia in 1874. In 1928, the Van Metre family sold the house to the board of trustees of the Columbia Township Auditorium, which wanted to build a large auditorium on the property. Columbia residents were outraged to discover the plans to destroy the home where President Wilson had spent part of his formative teenage years. Columbia's citizens banded together to save the property. In 1929, the house and the land were sold to the State of South Carolina to be preserved for future generations. The house operated as a museum and shrine to President Wilson by the state and then by the American Legion Auxiliary from 1932 until 1966. In 1966, the property was transferred to the Richland County Preservation Commission and jointly operated with Historic Columbia Foundation. Today, this nationally important site is undergoing a multiyear restoration that will return the structure to its 1872–74 appearance.

Local communities also banded together to create memorials to the individual soldiers from their neighborhoods who sacrificed for their country. The effort to establish a permanent memorial to the memory of the mill communities' fallen soldiers began during the spring of 1930, spearheaded by four local men. The local paper, the *Spinner*, ran a two-page article on the $2,000 monument in order to

This house was the boyhood family home of Woodrow Wilson. His time living in Columbia exposed him to Reconstruction-era life in the South, which impacted some of his presidential policies. Throughout the Great War, Columbians emphasized their connection to the president. *Courtesy Historic Columbia Foundation.*

solicit donations from the community. Fundraising efforts quickly raised $3,000 for the project, which was substantially more than the total cost of the statue. On an overcast November day, Reverend R.C. Griffith solemnly prayed to the crowd that had gathered for the monument's unveiling, "We pray to the God of Peace, that the time will come when all disagreements between nations will not be settled with gases and guns and when suspicion and fear and hate will give way to faith and hope and love." His voice echoed through the crowd that soberly gazed upon the monument dedicated in honor of eleven soldiers from the Pacific Mill Community during the Great War.[25]

The design of the monument portrays an American doughboy figure with a rifle, gas mask, helmet and hand grenade charging through barbed wire. These eleven men from one community in Columbia represented a disproportionate number of men who died in the war from South Carolina. These eleven men from the mill village stood for 18 percent of the white South Carolina soldiers who had died during the war, which was an exceptionally high mortality rate.

A bronze plaque on the front of the monument reads:

DEDICATED TO
THE MEMORY OF OUR
COMRADES
WHO GAVE THEIR LIVES IN
THE WORLD WAR

AUSTIN BARBER
HENRY BARFIELD
LADSON GALLOWAY
THOMAS J. LANGLEY
WALTER WEBB
FRANZ PROX
THOMAS MANUS
EDMUND DEKETELEARE
ROBERT MARTIN
WILLIAM SIMS
DAVIS GANTT

The monument also has inscribed on it the names of approximately 250 young men from the Pacific Mill Community who served in the war. The memorial reflects the gratitude of those in the community for the sacrifice and service of the local World War I soldiers. It expresses the honor of the men while reflecting the horror of trench warfare as the doughboy pushes through the barbed wire. The monument stands as a lasting tribute to those men and to the community that desired to honor them.[26]

In 1930, Columbia's Pacific Mill Community raised funds to erect this monument in memory of eleven men from the community who lost their lives while serving in the Great War. *Courtesy Historic Columbia Foundation.*

The war brought changes that dramatically altered Columbia's economic, social and built landscapes. Columbia's population dramatically increased and changed during the years surrounding the Great War. In 1900, the population of Richland County was 45,589. By 1920, the population rose to 78,122. Agricultural productivity also reached record levels. Although Camp Jackson officially closed on April 25, 1922, the camp brought new workers to the Columbia market. Local businesses advertised employment and educational opportunities to former soldiers. Furthermore, the camp's closure was only temporary, establishing the groundwork for it to become a major contributor to Columbia's economy when it permanently reopened during World War II. Currently, Fort Jackson employs 5,200 civilians and trains approximately 45,000 soldiers each year, adding a yearly estimated value of $6.2 billion to Columbia's economy.[27]

In spite of the horrors of trench warfare and the postwar diplomatic complications that would eventually lead America into the Second World War, many Columbians felt that these issues were overshadowed by the city's low military casualty rates and overall economic prosperity. Although the Spanish influenza had left its mark with fresh graves and weakened health, Columbia quickly returned to life as normal. Soon, the mass mobilization of the homefront required for World War II would overshadow the hardships endured during the Great War, almost erasing negative memories and emphasizing the supposed golden days of the city. In many ways, the Great War became a coming of age for Columbia after its devastation during the Civil War and before its transition into a suburbanite city. As Margaret Devereux eagerly emphasized when reflecting upon the city's Great War experiences, "I state categorically that there was and never will be, for us, such a Wonderful War again."[28]

The University of South Carolina in the Great War: Confronting Problems while Contributing to the War Effort

Elizabeth C. West, South Caroliniana Library,
University of South Carolina

A siren's song of glory and honor transfixed the students and alumni of the University of South Carolina during the Great War (1914–18), drawing them and the university into tumultuous times just when USC's future looked brighter than it had in decades. From 1880 to 1905, USC had undergone several reorganizations and name changes reflecting varying ideas of what its purpose and focus should be. The political and organizational turmoil in the late 1800s had caused enrollment to fluctuate severely, but at the turn of the century it had stabilized and then began to grow. Carolina was just beginning to develop into a modern university when a new crisis—war in Europe—appeared on the horizon.

At first, the war in Europe did not command the attention of the university administration and students, except as an occasional debate topic or inspiration for a work of fiction or poetry. In fact, the university administration feared that the United States' entry into the conflict would result in a mass exodus of students that would close down the university—which is what had happened during the Civil War. Therefore, President William S. Currell and the board of trustees tried to maintain a sense of normalcy at the university and initially opposed the establishment of a military training unit on campus. Currell declared, "While I believe in a reasonable amount of preparedness of a purely defensive character I am entirely averse to the spirit of militarism that seems to be in the air." In response to an inquiry in 1915 on the establishment of military training at USC, Currell stated, "I do not think it is probable that we shall reintroduce military training in the University of South Carolina as we already have two military training institutions, Clemson College...and The Citadel...which are giving very effective military drills and training."[1]

As the war dragged on and the pressure increased for the United States to enter it, interest grew in developing some sort of military training at the university. Currell reported to the board of trustees on June 12, 1916, that he had been approached "from several different angles" regarding the establishment of military training at Carolina.

William S. Currell served as the university's president from 1914 to 1922. *Courtesy University of South Carolina Archives.*

When Currell brought the matter before the executive committee of the board of trustees, they stated their opposition to compulsory training, but support for voluntary training under the instruction of a United States officer. Currell stated, "I am very much opposed to any form of compulsory military training at the university inasmuch as this runs counter to all of the traditions of the institution and I do not believe that any form of voluntary training can be made effective." Currell further stated his belief that the wave of militarism sweeping over the country would subside when the "European War" ended. However, he recommended that the board appoint a committee to investigate the issue.[2]

Currell seemed to have overlooked the military tradition at the institution. A cadet corps had been established at South Carolina College in 1825 in honor of the visit to Columbia by the Marquis de Lafayette. The cadets practiced drills and marched in the city parade. The corps remained on campus and even established an armory, with the trustees' permission. However, after a student riot in which the college's students seized the weapons and ammunition, the armory was closed and the corps members had to drill without their rifles. The corps died out when the majority of the student body left school to enlist in Confederate service in 1862, and it was not allowed to reform when the school reopened after the end of the Civil War.[3]

Six months after Currell stated his opposition to any form of military training at the university, he presented a report to the board of trustees on his investigations into establishing a reserve officers' training corps. The trustees' executive committee had instructed him to inquire on the procedures for introducing a military program. He stated, "While this would be a distinct innovation I believe it would be highly desirable not only because of the advantages of military training but because it is important to [align] the institution with the authorities of the National Government," since it was expected that the federal government would soon be distributing increasingly large expenditures on higher education and preparedness.[4]

At the start of 1917 Currell was making inquiries to the War Department regarding the regulations for establishing an ROTC unit. He also expressed interest in a pamphlet titled "Military Training for School Boys," since the university was "seriously contemplating the introduction of military features at the University of South Carolina."[5] Currell initially reported difficulties in securing information from the War Department, due to the "pressure of work" the department was under. However, he had received assurances from the secretary of war that the department would help set up a program if a suitable number of students was willing to take the training. He therefore recommended that the trustees vote on the wisdom of introducing military training at Carolina, leaving the details of developing that program to his committee, concluding, "The students are well nigh unanimous in their desire" to have such a program.[6]

Once the United States entered the war in April 1917, Currell and the trustees put aside their fears for Carolina's survival and fully supported the country's war efforts, even though those efforts were sometimes detrimental to the university's operation. That month, the board approved the establishment of a military training unit. The first unit was an unofficial voluntary program headed by retired General Hugh Thompson, who refused payment for his services, which he felt honor-bound to supply. This was a

In July 1917, President William S. Currell traveled to the reserve officers' training camp held at Chickamauga Park, Georgia, to deliver diplomas to the university's seniors. *Courtesy University of South Carolina Archives.*

ROTC students in 1918 pose in front of Barnwell College, then named LeConte College. *Courtesy University of South Carolina Archives.*

make-do program until the War Department could provide an active military officer to head an official ROTC unit. Nearly three-fourths of the student body joined. By August the program had been officially established as a Reserve Officer Training Corps with Colonel H.C. Davis as professor of military science and tactics. The military training was compulsory for freshmen and sophomores and voluntary for other students.[7]

Additional military training was established at colleges and universities in September 1918 via the Student Army Training Corps. SATC students were members of the United States Army, but were on furlough status and without pay until called to duty. All members over the age of eighteen in the SATC were subject to active service at the call of the president. Training was performed by regular army officers. The army wanted college graduates for officers, and the SATC would prevent "unnecessary and wasteful depletion of the colleges through indiscriminate volunteering by offering to the students a definite and immediate military status," while developing a large body of college students in a military asset.[8] In addition to the SATC students, the university's enrollment was helped by the decision to admit more female

ROTC students undergo physical training on Gibbes Green, circa 1918. *Courtesy University of South Carolina Archives.*

Women were not allowed in the ROTC, but they did serve at home and overseas in the Red Cross. The university offered Red Cross classes during the war to help meet the demand for this type of training. *Courtesy University of South Carolina Archives.*

students. Although the women were not allowed in the ROTC at that time, they were able to participate in the war effort through the YWCA and the Red Cross, which held classes at USC during the war years.[9]

With the majority of the students enrolled in the ROTC and the addition of the SATC, the campus resembled an army training camp, thus alleviating the administration's fears that the war would force the school's closing. However, the university did experience difficulties in continuing normal academic operations as the war effort siphoned off faculty members. President Currell recommended that faculty members who either volunteered or were called into service be allowed a leave of absence, and that their positions be temporarily filled with substitutes and be open to them upon their discharge.[10]

By 1918, nearly half of USC's faculty members were on leaves of absence to participate in wartime activities. Throughout the war, telegrams from the War Department arrived on Currell's desk requesting the immediate services of a particular professor. Each request was approved, despite the crippling effect this practice had on USC's teaching effectiveness. To do otherwise could invite charges of being unpatriotic.

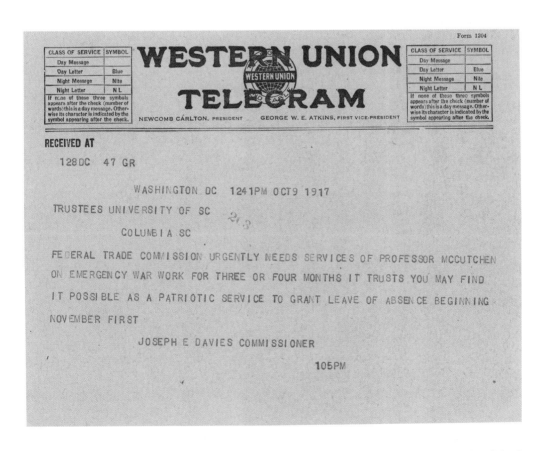

Each telegram like this one meant another reshuffling of teaching duties. *Courtesy University of South Carolina Archives.*

Among faculty members serving in the war were psychology and philosophy professor Josiah Morse and economics professor George McCutchen. Morse was often away from campus serving as the director for the Red Cross activities in South Carolina, while McCutchen was called away to assist the Federal Trade Commission.[11] A number of professors went through military training to be able to teach in the SATC program. One of these was Professor Oscar L. Keith, who taught modern languages. Of this training, Keith wrote, "Strong muscles and strong language are recommended by the officers...and swearing and sweating are in the order of the day."[12]

Like the university's administration, Carolina's students at first were opposed to entering the war. Initially, the European conflict was limited to academic discussions and debates. Student debates were a long-held tradition at the University of South Carolina, dating back to the institution's opening. The members of the Clariosophic and Euphradian Literary Societies, established in 1806 as debating organizations, had covered a wide range of local, state and national topics over the decades, including taxes, politics, slavery, women's rights and war. The Great War first appeared as a debate topic in September 1914, when the Clariosophics asked whether the United States should intercede in order to bring about the cessation of hostilities in the crisis; the debate was decided in the negative.[13] The Clariosophics were silent on the conflict until one year later, when they decided in the affirmative that the United States should enact a law prohibiting the exportation of arms to the belligerents and that the Allies and the Central Powers held equal responsibility in starting the conflict.[14]

But the closer the United States came to entering the war, the more the students came to look upon it as a great adventure promising glory and honor. Their romanticized view of the war was evident in the

Josiah Morse, professor of psychology and philosophy, served as director of the Red Cross activities in South Carolina and helped institute Red Cross courses at USC. *Courtesy University of South Carolina Archives.*

This 1918 photograph shows the officers of the Student Army Training Corps at USC. Professor Oscar L. Keith is in the center of the middle row. *Courtesy of University of South Carolina Archives.*

articles, poetry and artwork they produced in campus publications, most notably in the *Carolinian*. The literary societies began publishing the *Carolinian* in 1883. Although it did carry a few brief news items and editorials, its main purpose was to provide a forum for student fiction and poetry, usually of the moonlight and magnolias style. The war-related writings were no different, full of battlefield glory, honorable soldiers and tragic wartime romances. Student poetry was flushed with excitement, patriotism and eagerness to participate in the great adventure. Among the poems was one that specifically addressed the effects of the war on the University of South Carolina. Another poem, titled "April 1917," appeared in both the *Carolinian* and the *Garnet and Black* yearbook and won the *Carolinian* medal for best poem published in 1917.

> *I long to stand today where life and death*
> *Are met as one, where from the boundless sky*
> *On unseen wings war's eagles scream and sweep,*
> *Where charging men in the long grey lines stampede*

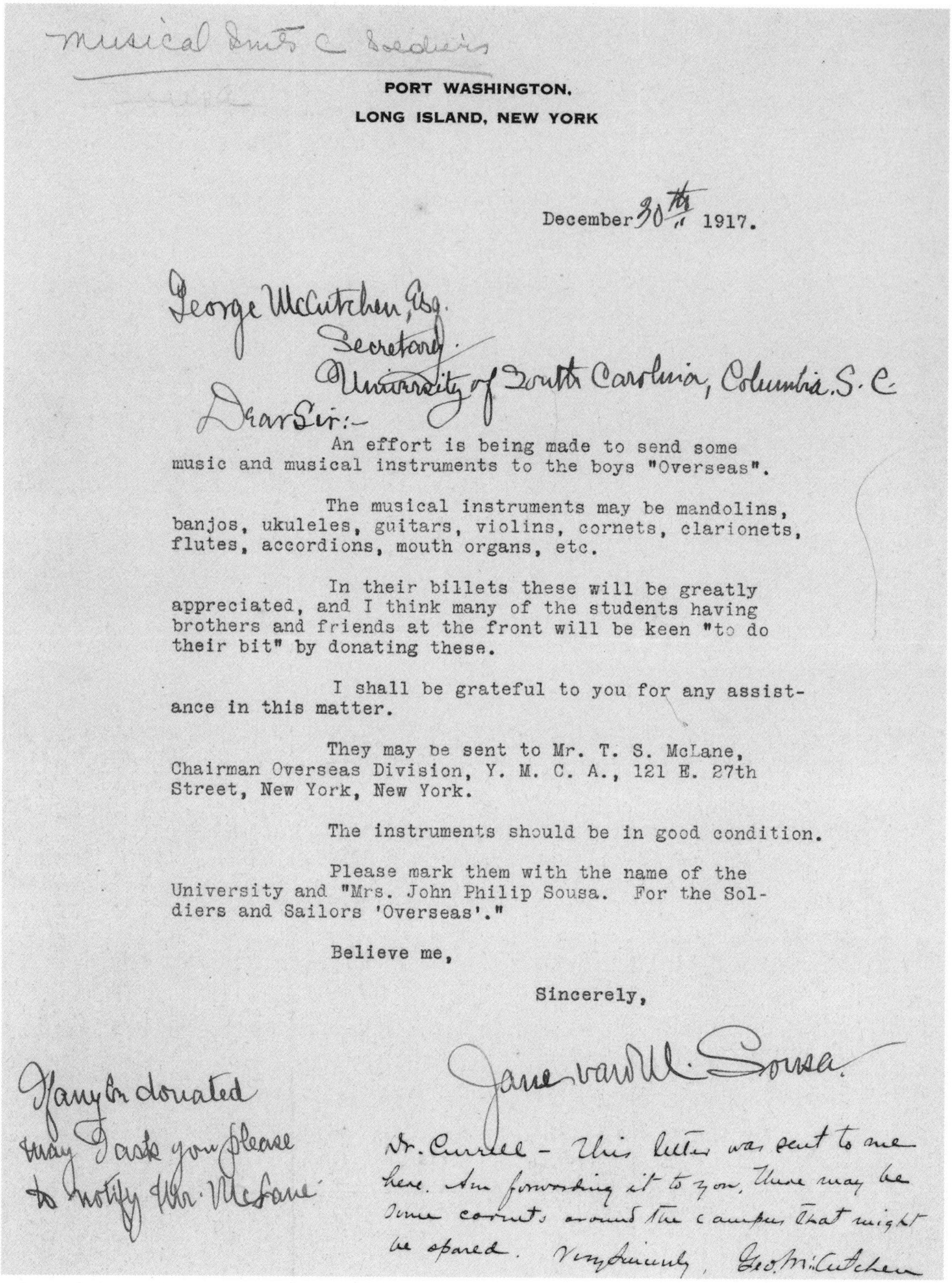

musical instruments & soldiers

PORT WASHINGTON,
LONG ISLAND, NEW YORK

December 30th 1917.

George McCutchen, Esq.
　　Secretary.
　　University of South Carolina, Columbia, S. C.

Dear Sir:—

An effort is being made to send some
music and musical instruments to the boys "Overseas".

The musical instruments may be mandolins,
banjos, ukuleles, guitars, violins, cornets, clarionets,
flutes, accordions, mouth organs, etc.

In their billets these will be greatly
appreciated, and I think many of the students having
brothers and friends at the front will be keen "to do
their bit" by donating these.

I shall be grateful to you for any assistance in this matter.

They may be sent to Mr. T. S. McLane,
Chairman Overseas Division, Y. M. C. A., 121 E. 27th
Street, New York, New York.

The instruments should be in good condition.

Please mark them with the name of the
University and "Mrs. John Philip Sousa. For the Soldiers and Sailors 'Overseas'."

Believe me,

Sincerely,

Jane van M. Sousa

If any be donated
may I ask you please
to notify Mr. McLane

Dr. Currell — This letter was sent to me
here. Am forwarding it to you. There may be
some cornets around the campus that might
be spared. Very sincerely, Geo. McCutchen

The wife of composer and conductor John Philip Sousa wrote to Carolina and other universities asking for the donation of used musical instruments to help boost the morale of troops. *Courtesy University of South Carolina Archives.*

Across the rugged hills that timid Spring
Now fears to heap with her accustomed flowers.

Ah, I have tasted life and found its waters
A bitter mockery, so flat and stale!
Better to drink of war's red-flaming cup
For but a day, to feel life's stream at last
Come pulsing firm and strong, than for an age
To live the bonded slave of Circumstance![15]

Among the short stories were tragic romances, including a soldier who hastily married his sweetheart before shipping out, only to find true love with a French girl he could not have; a soldier who died in a trench clutching the photograph of "a beautifully sad French girl"; and a courtship that led to a wedding, only to have German bombs destroy the church during the ceremony, killing everyone inside.[16] A different kind of tragic tale was that of Marquis, published in the April 1917 issue. The story presents the tale of the training, service and death of a Red Cross assistance dog.

Poor, faithful, loving Marquis! Blood was gushing from the hole in his chest but he crawled slowly back to the now still and silent figure under the plane. There he lay quite a while,

Patriotic bunting decorated the gymnasium for various events, including this image of the German Club from the 1918 *Garnet and Black* yearbook. The club was named for a type of dance, not the country. *Courtesy University of South Carolina Archives.*

The Men of Carolina
(Published in the *Carolinian*, December 1917)

There's a hush upon the campus now and thru the dusty halls,
There's a silence now, no more the air resounds with happy calls.
Across the pleasant green sward more youthful figures stray,
For the Men of Carolina have gaily marched away.

No more within the lecture rooms they hear the learned lore
Of bygone hours, of greater men, the dreams they dreamed before,
For their eyes have caught the vision, they were dazzled by its gleam,
And the Men of Carolina shall perpetuate our dream.

And out upon the campus now are figures dimly seen
Clad in their suits of somber gray, they march upon the green,
So indistinct, so shadowy, that none may dream or know.
They're the Men of Carolina who marched out long ago.

They are the men in bygone year fell on Virginia's plain,
But they know their strength is needed, so they're coming back again.
And filled with that brave spirit, just as it used to be,
The men of seventeen can hear the call of sixty-three.

The Men of Carolina! Let's give them greeting high,
The martial sons of martial race who know to live and die,
For when the call was sounded to bear the battle's brunt,
The Men of Carolina marched bravely to the front.

They've marched away in joyousness, with a cheery laugh and smile,
Tho they know that they'll be leaving now for such a bitter while.
But they heard the battle's echoes where is thundered from afar
And the Men of Carolina have marched away to war.

And if they fall into battle, the you who stay behind,
You sons of Carolina, must bear their fame in mind,
And keep forever glowing the lamp that they did light,
The Men of Carolina—who marched away to fight.

The Men of Carolina! God keep their scutcheon clean
From any stain of Cowardice as it has ever been.
God greet them, merry gentlemen, so gaily marching by,
The Men of Carolina—For they're marching out—to die!

—E.R. Jeter

his nose just touching the neck of his beloved master. From time to time he would raise his head and caress that cold, damp forehead with his tongue. Then soon he too became still.

The guns on both sides that flashed and roared all night long and the glaring lights that flared and lit up the surroundings from time to time revealed a scene of disturbed peace in the little hole in the forest of "no man's land." There two soldiers were dead.[17]

The *Garnet and Black* yearbook also reflected the students' patriotic fervor with red, white and blue artwork; images of the ROTC, SATC and wartime activities; and articles on how faculty and alumni were serving the war effort. The 1918 edition was dedicated to "men who exalt honor above security, liberty above life, humanity above self." Students also demonstrated their patriotism by decorating for many social events, such as dances, with the colors of the flag.[18]

Carolina's administrators attempted to keep track of the school's former students who were serving in armed forces. Over five hundred Carolina alumni served, and each of

—Drawn By A. O. V. Hoffman.   His First Bow.

"PAR-LAY VOO FRAWN-SAY?"—PAGE 20.

Students often saw humor in the experiences of American soldiers in France, as in this illustration by A.O.V. Hoffman (class of 1918) for a story about a Southern soldier's efforts to charm a French woman. It was published in the January 1918 *Carolinian. Courtesy University of South Carolina Archives.*

Patriotic artwork from the 1919 *Garnet and Black* yearbook. *Courtesy University of South Carolina Archives.*

Artwork above the university's library from the 1919 *Garnet and Black* yearbook depicting a battle scene. *Courtesy University of South Carolina Archives.*

them had a star on the university's own blue star service flag, which was displayed in Rutledge Chapel during the war.[19] University records do not indicate what happened to the flag afterward. Several of the twenty-eight alumni who died during the war were killed in action.

Samuel Turtletaub, who left before completing his degree in 1916, was cited for the Distinguished Service Cross for heroism displayed. He was killed in battle in France on September 29, 1918. Robert O. Purdy Jr. (class of 1914) had been gassed and wounded in previous engagements before being killed on July 19, 1918, while leading his platoon in France. John M. McIntosh (class of 1916) was described in the 1916 *Garnet and Black* as follows: "In his work he succeeds well, doing in his own quiet way the thing that has to be done." He died on September 12, 1918, while leading his men against a machine gun nest. He was posthumously cited for bravery.[20] Other alumni in the service succumbed to diseases, including the influenza pandemic that struck in 1918, forcing the university to be quarantined for a week. Several students in the SATC died of flu-related pneumonia.[21]

Lieut. Samuel D. Turtletaub

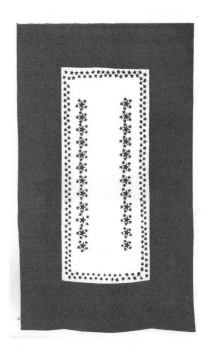

Left: Samuel Turteltaub. *Courtesy University of South Carolina Archives.*

Right: The University Service Flag hung in Rutledge Chapel during the war. Each star sewn on the flag represents a Carolina alumnus in the service of his country. Surviving university records do not indicate what happened to the flag after the war. *Courtesy University of South Carolina Archives.*

After the armistice was signed on November 11, 1918, Carolina settled back into normal civilian collegiate activities and support for keeping military training in peacetime waned. The SATC had been disbanded immediately after the war ended, and many of the university's administrators, supporters and students saw no need to retain military training on campus. In 1921, the board of trustees abolished the ROTC program, stating it was "inconsistent with the tradition of the University."[22]

In the years following the war, Carolina welcomed back many students who had withdrawn from school to serve their country. Other veterans entered the university for the first time, including Medal of Honor recipient Richmond H. Hilton (class of 1924). Hilton earned the Medal of Honor for his actions in battle. In leading an attack on a machine gun nest, Hilton advanced well ahead of his men and personally killed six of the enemy and captured ten. The wounds he received during this action resulted in the loss of an arm.[23] After graduating from USC, he practiced law in Camden until his death by drowning in 1933. Some of the returning veterans were destined to be leaders in South Carolina government, including future Speaker of the House Solomon Blatt and future Governor and United States Senator Olin D. Johnston.

John S. Reynolds Jr.

John S. Reynolds Jr. was one of the over five hundred Carolina alumni who entered military service during World War I. Reynolds, a bright, cheerful young man known for his keen intellect, began working at the *State* newspaper while still a student at the University of South Carolina. After his graduation in 1907, he continued with the newspaper, quickly advancing through the ranks to become news editor—the second-highest-ranking position on the editorial staff. During the eight months preceding America's entry into the war, and for four months afterward, Reynolds penned the majority of the war-related editorials in the *State*.[1] When the United States entered the conflict, Reynolds never hesitated when it came time to lay down the pen and pick up the sword, stating, "Having written these editorials in favor of the war, I must do my duty as a soldier; I shall have to live with myself, you know."[2]

After graduating from the officers' training camp at Fort Oglethorpe, Georgia, in November 1917, Reynolds was assigned to the Third Infantry Division, U.S. Army.[3] He

married sweetheart Emily Bellinger shortly thereafter, but like many other wartime newlyweds they enjoyed only a few weeks together before Reynolds reported for duty. This couple was fortunate, however, in that John was stationed nearby at Camp Greene, North Carolina, allowing for visits by his new bride, including a sort of second honeymoon. On April 2, 1918, Reynolds's regiment sailed out of New York Harbor.[4]

John S. Reynolds Jr. *Courtesy John S. Reynolds Jr. Papers, South Caroliniana Library, University of South Carolina.*

His letters from the front describe the daily routines of army life, the French people and countryside and, most prominently, his love for Emily: "Your name comes from my soul to my lips—to remain unuttered—a thousand times a day, whether in the hot rain of shot and shell, or in the cold rain of nature, in the bright camp days or the dreary, dripping marches."[5] Although the letters sent to Reynolds from his wife, mother and other relatives are no longer extant, it is apparent from his replies to them that they pressed for more details on military life and the war. Citing strict rules of censorship that forbade him from complying, Reynolds nonetheless expressed the fear that his letters were monotonous and disappointing, telling his mother, "It's as if in laying aside the pen for the sword...I had lost all skill with the former."[6] In a letter dated August 6, 1918, however, Reynolds finally provided his wife with a detailed description of his experience, the only time he would do so.

> We were in a wood, in shelters digged in the ground, when our own guns heralded the battle with a fierce counterbarrage—a counterbarrage as effective as it was welcome to us. Then came the enemy's fire and for hours the wood rocked and groaned under the hail of shell as if some terrific storm were sweeping it and continually hurling into its midst the flashing terrible lightenings which blast and burn.[7]

On September 26, Reynolds's regiment deployed to the Bois de Sivry, the same morning that the Allies began the Meuse-Argonne offensive. On October 9, Reynolds's platoon participated in fierce combat, moving into a heavy barrage of high explosive shells and then into the teeth of German machine guns. He took a hand grenade and an automatic pistol and killed three Germans manning a machine gun nest. Reynolds himself was wounded in both legs.[8] As he was transported to an aid station, he maintained a cheerfulness and apologized to the men carrying him for causing them trouble. He also wondered if his wounds were severe enough to cause him to be evacuated.[9]

On November 24, 1918, Joan Schreiner Reynolds was born, just days before her parents' first wedding anniversary. Thanksgiving and Christmas passed with no word from her father. Finally, letters arrived from his chaplain and a fellow officer. Emily found out about his death from those who had served with him. She asked John's dear friend and coworker, William Watts Ball, to contact the army for official confirmation. On January 7, 1919, she received a telegram confirming the death of First Lieutenant John S. Reynolds Jr. He had died on the operating table on October 10, seven weeks before his only child was born.[10] A few days before the battle that cost him his life, John Reynolds wrote his final letter to Emily.

Reynolds's final letter to his wife. *Courtesy John S. Reynolds Jr. Papers, South Caroliniana Library, University of South Carolina.*

Sweetheart:

I haven't time tonight for much—duties are pressing and moments fleeting— but I can't let another day pass, darling, without telling you once again the old, old story, that I love you today and tomorrow and ever, world without end... Infinitely sweet it has been to have you; infinitely sweet it is to feel that some day, when our parting time is over, we shall be together for a long lifetime and forever and forever after that.

Oh, love, the only star of my soul, the only flower in the wide world for me, you can hardly know—even you—how full my heart is of you, daily and nightly...that our love is to be crowned in that new life—new love—that is to enter into it makes it all the sweeter, all the more worthwhile....Now, dear heart, I'll say goodbye, with love to the family and a whole everlasting soul full for you, my bride, my love, my only girl—best and bravest and sweetest of wives.

Yours, John[11]

---

1. *State*, January 4, 1919.

2. Ibid.

3. Ibid.

4. Typescript, history of the Thirtieth Regiment, Reynolds Papers. Author unknown. This document appears to be the basis for the Thirtieth Regiment's section in the published history of the Third Infantry Division.

5. John S. Reynolds Jr. to Emily Reynolds, August 6, 1918. John Schreiner Reynolds Jr. Papers, Manuscripts Division, South Caroliniana Library, University of South Carolina, Columbia.

6. Reynolds to Susan Edwards Reynolds, May 12, 1918.

7. Reynolds to Emily Reynolds, August 6, 1918.

8. Captain H.A. Amber to Emily Reynolds, August 29, 1919.

9. Chaplain George W. Sadler to Clarkson, November 25, 1918.

10. *State*, January 8, 1919.

11. Reynolds to Emily Reynolds, October 3, 1918.

G. E. Shand, Jr., Captain

Gadsden E. Shand Jr. (class of 1918) is shown here in his uniform as captain of C Company, ROTC. Shand helped care for many sick students during the influenza pandemic of 1918. *Courtesy University of South Carolina Archives.*

The university made several efforts to memorialize those who died in military service during the Great War, but not all of them have survived the subsequent decades. On April 29, 1919, USC held a memorial service in which elm trees were planted as living memorials for each of the twenty-eight deceased alumni. In 1923 a plaque honoring the twenty-eight deceased Carolinians was placed at the front entrance of the South Caroliniana Library, where it remains today. In 1927, the American Legion Auxiliary sponsored the placement of markers at the bases of the elms as well as a large granite boulder on Greene Street near Melton Observatory to honor surviving veterans.[24] However, as the campus landscape changed over the years, many of the elm trees died and the markers were removed or destroyed. Only five markers remain on the Pickens Street side of Hamilton College.

Although Carolina's campus is the location of the city's most prominent Great War memorial, the university did not actually build the structure. The World War Memorial Building was constructed in 1935 to honor all South Carolinians who served and died during the Great War. The War Memorial Commission and the Historical Commission of South Carolina directed its construction, which was raised through private subscriptions and a federal grant from the Works Progress Administration. The university's board of trustees donated the use of the land at the corner of Sumter and Greene Streets, which required moving a university building, Flinn Hall, back approximately fifty yards to its present location.[25] Among the agencies housed by the War Memorial were the South Carolina Department of Archives and History and the Confederate Relic Room and Military Museum, since the university owned the land but not the building. Ownership of the building recently was transferred to the university, and the structure was renovated to house University Publications. It is no longer open to the public.

Military training did not find a permanent place at Carolina until the establishment of the Naval ROTC in 1940, when another world war would once again strain the

Richmond H. Hilton. *Courtesy University of South Carolina Archives.*

This stone marker for Samuel Turteltaub is one of the few remaining in its original location. *Courtesy University of South Carolina Archives.*

university's normal operations by transforming it yet again into a military training camp. This time, the ROTC would remain a permanent fixture on campus. The Air Force ROTC was added in 1949, and after almost sixty years, the Army ROTC finally returned to Carolina in 1980.[26]

However, the most lasting impact of the Great War on the University of South Carolina was in the makeup of the student body. Prior to World War I, only a handful of women attended the university. Administrators were not enthusiastic about coeducation, and the institution did not offer on-campus housing for women. However, in an effort to cope with the loss of male students to the military, the administration decided to admit more female students during World War I, and a wing of DeSaussure College was converted into women's housing. After the war, the number of female students continued to slowly climb until the university was finally forced to construct the first women's dormitory in 1924.[27] This gradual increase in their numbers that began during the Great War gave a stronger foothold to the fledgling coeducation movement at Carolina. Their numbers continued to grow in the following decades, so much so that since 1981 there have been more female students than male.[28]

SOUTH CAROLINA SOLDIERS AND UNITS ON THE WESTERN FRONT

Joe Long, South Carolina Confederate
Relic Room and Military Museum

South Carolina Prepares for War

A state with a strong martial tradition, South Carolina provided as many soldiers for Great War service as the state had for the Confederate army a half-century earlier. With America's entry into the First World War, the state once more underwent a mobilization of manpower and resources of titanic proportions. South Carolina's military heritage was reinvigorated for participation in the nation's war effort, this time in a world struggle.

In 1917 as the United States entered the great European war, the nation accepted unprecedented alliances with European powers and took on a new and daunting role on the world stage. For the state of South Carolina, the federalization of its national guard and the state's commitment to the national war effort were also drastic steps and a shift of perspective from regional to international affairs. In Woodrow Wilson and Benjamin Baruch, our state contributed two of the leaders who enabled national mobilization, but ordinary South Carolina families and private soldiers would prove equally vital to the eventual achievement of Allied victory.

The war also foreshadowed social changes to come later in the century. Black and white participants both experienced combat and interacted with French society during the war, and found many Jim Crow–era assumptions challenged in the course of their service. At home the inclusion of African Americans in the nation's military plan was a source of debate, and even homefront support for the war effort was divided on racial lines. Meanwhile, though segregated from one another, black and white South Carolinians served gallantly as United States soldiers and established parallel legacies in the world struggle they had been drawn into.

South Carolina would not only prepare itself for its role in the struggle, but also play a disproportionate part in the preparation of the American Expeditionary Force as a whole. Forty-two thousand American servicemen were trained at Camp Jackson alone, and South Carolina's provision of basic training sites for the armed forces would continue through the twentieth century and to the current day.

British brodie-style helmet of Private First Class Clyde McTeer, 120th Infantry, 30th Division. The helmet emblem is the 30th Division "Old Hickory" symbol. *Courtesy South Carolina Confederate Relic Room and Military Museum.*

Mexican Border Campaign

As regards Mexico, the President seems to hint that intervention may also be the mother of necessity.
—*South Carolina Sergeant Robert Gonzales*[1]

While the European powers struggled for supremacy, another war raged much closer to home. Revolutionary factions struggled for the control of Mexico, and President Wilson's administration watched events south of the Rio Grande with growing alarm. When the town of Columbus, New Mexico, was raided by revolutionaries under Mexican leader Pancho Villa, Wilson mobilized state militia troops to protect American citizens and property in the Southwest.

Campaign hat of Sergeant Jesse Barton, quartermaster corps. Campaign hats were worn during Mexican border service and at the beginning of U.S. involvement in World War I. The garrison-style cap later replaced the campaign hat. *Courtesy South Carolina Confederate Relic Room and Military Museum.*

South Carolina Soldiers and Units on the Western Front

For South Carolina troops, this security duty along the Mexican border provided a significant prologue to the Great War. South Carolina troops served there alongside the regular U.S. Army, safeguarding United States citizens and property against the depredations of Pancho Villa's marauding revolutionaries. South Carolina's First and Second Infantries, as well as South Carolina Field Hospital Number One and Troop A of the South Carolina Cavalry (the Charleston Light Dragoons), went to the Mexican border and served for much of 1916, returning in December of that year.

For the soldiers this expedition involved national honor, and for many it also appealed to a sense of adventure. Headed for the Wild West in their distinctive broad-brimmed campaign hats, they would quickly learn that tedium as well as danger awaited in the field. They were also drawn closer to the struggle in Europe, as German diplomatic machinations in Mexico resulted in American outrage.

Both the South Carolina regiments and the regular army gained invaluable field experience from the Mexican campaign. Logistical challenges had to be met, and opportunities for employing new military methods were found. General John J. Pershing, who would command the AEF in Europe, led the Punitive Expedition sent into Mexico to apprehend General Francisco Pancho Villa. The American soldiers would experience misery and frustration pursuing the elusive revolutionary. However, such elements of the campaign as the use of aircraft for reconnaissance would help the U.S. Army begin to catch up with the fast-developing technology the European armies were already incorporating in their war. Frontier methods were incorporated with modern weapons, as mules were used to transport machine guns and aircraft reconnaissance was augmented by the use of Native American scouts on horseback.

Image from Mexican border service; the Second South Carolina Band just finished playing "Somewhere a Voice is Calling." *Courtesy Robert L. Brown.*

On a more personal level, South Carolina's troops learned that even a deployment like this would take its toll—the popular South Carolina newspaper columnist Robert Gonzales died of disease while serving as a noncommissioned officer on the border. Soldiers saw as well the aftermath of Mexican Revolution combat with automatic weapons and twentieth-century tactics. It proved to be a mere foretaste of the horrors in which they would soon be immersed.

During the Punitive Expedition the state volunteer system was employed for the last time, with each state's troops serving in their state militia regiments. When the same troops were called up for World War I, they would be reorganized, their units redesignated and made part of the regular army.

Mobilization and Draft

Upon their return from the border intervention, South Carolina's citizen-soldiers soon found themselves preparing for deployment to France. When war with Germany was declared in April, South Carolina's troops were called up for the defense of the state. That summer, however, they were summoned into federal service. In the reorganization that followed the activation of the national guard for federal service, the 1st South Carolina Regiment became the 118th Infantry. Assigned to the 30th ("Old Hickory") Division, the 118th would become one of the most distinguished regiments of the AEF. It was joined in the 30th Division by Troop A of the South Carolina cavalry (which became "Headquarters Troop") and by the Field Hospital that had deployed to the Mexican border. Meanwhile, the 2nd South Carolina Infantry became the 105th Ammunition Train, giving the 30th Division logistical support.

Activation of the national guard on July 25, 1917, had doubled the size of the United States Army, but even this expansion was insufficient to hope to realistically affect the course of the European war. Another more controversial policy followed: the national draft. For the first time since the desperate days of the Confederacy, South Carolina men were subject to conscription. Draftees were organized into the national army, distinguished from both the regular army and the national guard. This national army also included the segregated troops of the 93rd Division, whose 371st Regiment was composed primarily of African American South Carolinians.

South Carolinians would also serve in great numbers in many other units, including especially the 81st ("Wildcat") and 42nd ("Rainbow") Divisions. In fact, among the first to France were the 117th Engineers, commanded by Colonel James Johnson of Marion, South Carolina. South Carolinians would be found among the marines and sailors serving overseas as well.

The newly expanded army had to be trained and equipped, and major South Carolina contributions to this process occurred at the training bases Camp Jackson and Camp Sevier. Here recruits became soldiers, as the army attempted to prepare for battle in the conditions of European trench warfare. "Peacetime warfare," as one officer referred to the conditions of Mexican border service, was left behind. French

Field medical kit of Sergeant William H. Greene, Field Hospital 119, 105th Sanitary Train, 30th Division. Greene served on the Mexican border before World War I. *Courtesy South Carolina Confederate Relic Room and Military Museum.*

and British instructors undertook the deadly serious task of inculcating the skills vital to survival and victory on the Western Front.

Patriotic Homefront Efforts

American society adjusted to the new experience of total war. The mobilization, not just of the military, but of society at large, reminded older South Carolinians of their homefront experiences in the Confederate period. Ladies at home once more formed associations to provide knitted goods for the soldiers at the front, and Confederate monuments reminded a new generation of war's terrible toll. New organizations such as the American Red Cross helped organize the traditional homefront support on modern organizational lines, while organizations commemorating past conflicts joined in. The Red Cross, first founded in 1881, truly came into its own during World War I. With facilities on both sides of the Atlantic and the engagement of twenty million

Trousers, tunic, Sam Browne belt and service cap of Captain Ernest H. Capplemann, 323rd Infantry, 81st Division. *Courtesy South Carolina Confederate Relic Room and Military Museum.*

American adults as volunteers, the Red Cross mobilized civilian efforts with great efficiency. Its programs provided an outlet for both civilian patriotism and humanitarian impulses, which were directed to the war effort and the relief of the war's casualties. Red Cross nurses traveled overseas, as did their counterparts in the YMCA, providing visible assistance near the front itself while their organizations continued to focus civilian support efforts on the homefront. Warm knitted goods were provided to the soldiers at war by women's associations at home, just as they had been during the 1860s. Both sentimental and practical in nature, these gifts were much appreciated. However, homefront organizers soon found contributions to make beyond this traditional activity, as the nation's economic resources were fully mobilized.

It was a great satisfaction to find our dear old Memorial women ready to enlist to do whatever was possible—to sew, to knit, to care for our boys—just as they did in the sixties. For the first time in the history of this country the women are asked to take part in financial affairs. We are asked to form liberty loan committees within our Associations; we are asked to invest all available funds in the purchase of liberty bonds...If you cannot buy a bond, buy war savings stamps...everybody, old and young, rich and poor can subscribe, and must do so if they are true Americans.[2]

The United Daughters of the Confederacy of South Carolina mobilized their resources for the support of South Carolina's soldiers. Taking a lead role was

Mrs. Carolina Girardeau, assistant "Custodian" (curator) for the Confederate Relic Room in Columbia. Mrs. Girardeau had two sons serving in the Allied forces, and was one of the founding members of Columbia's Red Cross. The "canteen corps" she helped establish provided food and encouragement for recruits on trains on the way to Camp Jackson and veterans returning home. She also manned a free recreation center located at the corner of Main and Taylor Streets in Columbia.[3]

The Daughters of the Confederacy strove to perpetuate the Confederate legacy among the American soldiers, particularly those with familial ties to Confederate soldiers. "The Brave Begat the Brave" read the Latin inscription on the UDC Cross of Service, the medal that the Daughters awarded to those descendants of Confederate soldiers who now fought in the "Great War for Civilization." Rhapsodized one Daughter,

> *The cause of Lee and Jackson, though 'twas trampled in the dust*
> *By overwhelming odds, has risen, commanding world-wide trust;*
> *'Tis now the cause of Pershing and his brave boys o'er the sea,*
> *The cause upheld by Dixie's knights with Jackson and with Lee.*[4]

Swift to capitalize on this martial spirit, America's French allies dispatched the Marquise de Courtivron to visit the Southern states in January of 1918. Helene Agnes de Courtivron was a daughter of Confederate General de Polignac, and her goodwill tour began in Charleston and continued with a formal presentation of her father's sword to the state of Virginia. Charleston's UDC Chapter awarded de Courtivron membership and coordinated with her to endow seventy beds in the American Military Hospital in Neuilly, France, in the organization's name.[5] De Courtivron "promised that it would be her duty and pleasure to look after the comfort of any American boy who may occupy the Wade Hampton bed established by the South Carolina Division in the American Military hospital" in Neuilly.[6]

Many prominent South Carolina soldiers qualified for the UDC Cross of Service. Major General John Murray Jenkins, son of Confederate General Micah Jenkins, was a brigade commander in the Meuse-Argonne offensive and suffered poison gas damage three times; he was awarded a Distinguished Service Cross by the army. Major Harrison Saunders, commanding the 12th Aero Squadron, was a grandson of Confederate surgeon William Anderson. Corporal James Heriot was the grandson of Confederate Captain Robert Chandler, and one of three Medal of Honor winners from the 118th Infantry Regiment to qualify for the UDC Cross of Service as well.

Confederate veterans, so familiar with the danger and misery of war, were also prominent in their support of the "war to end wars." Indeed the Sons of Confederate Veterans organization took part in a national Preparedness Parade in Washington, D.C., in June 1916. The organization passed resolutions at the year's national convention "approving the preparedness program and offering their services to the United States."[7]

Toque of Captain Ernest Cappelmann, 323rd Infantry, 81st Division. This knitted cap served as cold weather headgear. Women on the homefront as well as outside contractors made knitted goods. The Red Cross distributed knitted items made on the homefront. *Courtesy South Carolina Confederate Relic Room and Military Museum.*

Naval Transport of Troops

"Out of sight, out of mind" doesn't apply to the submarine.
—Sergeant Robert Gonzales[8]

U.S. forces faced logistic challenges and physical hazards before even arriving in Europe. The Kaiser had been willing to provoke the United States into war partly because of assurances he received from his generals that no American army could successfully negotiate the U-boat-infested Atlantic in time to affect the outcome of the struggle.

Indeed, United States soldiers did not cross the Atlantic in significant numbers until the spring of 1918, the final year of the war. However, troop transport was little hampered by the vaunted German submarines. Still, the U-boat menace added to the anxieties of the soldiers who crowded onto waiting transports, segregated by rank and race, and forbidden even to remove their cumbersome life jackets during the transatlantic ordeal.

Sergeant Julius Hubbard had pointed opinions on the transportation effort:

> *As long as the American soldiers who were aboard the SS* Mongolia *live, they will never forgive the officials responsible for our treatment and a certain amount of hatred will always exist not because conditions were as they were but because not a man turned a hand to better them...The food was worse than you could conceive of and even its odor was sickening. Men were not allowed to remove their life belts or any part of their clothing, day or night, and were packed in sleeping quarters worse than any animals have ever been brought "overseas." The officers lived like kings, private staterooms, baths...I was not sorry for myself, but for the other men.*[9]

The U-boats were unable to seriously hamper troop transport, however, and soon an American army was preparing to fight on European soil.

When the troops arrived in France, they would be issued garrison caps, which were far more convenient for carry—an important consideration since much of their front-line time would be spent wearing helmets. They were also delivered to British and French instructors for a final round of intensive training before being sent into battle.

318th Field Artillery Band

Military musicians played an important part in encouraging patriotism, and sometimes in relieving the misery. They also found themselves serving in a diplomatic role at times, as music was an expected feature of ceremonies. All three roles were played by the men of the 318th Field Artillery Band.

The 318th Field Artillery Band had originally been organized in Orangeburg, South Carolina, in 1907 and had served in the Mexican border deployment as militia soldiers before being reorganized as a U.S. Army band with the AEF. Originally it had been the band of the 2nd South Carolina Infantry Regiment. General Pershing complimented

Hand-painted banner presented to the 318th Field Artillery Band from the people of Nice, France. *Courtesy South Carolina Confederate Relic Room and Military Museum.*

the unit personally during their deployment to the Southwest, and made use of them in France as well.

A signature tune for the band was "Somewhere a Voice is Calling": "Dusk and the shadows falling o'er land and sea, Somewhere a voice is calling, calling for me."

On the Mexican border after a concert, Captain Robert Brown noted in his scrapbook, "The band has just finished playing 'Somewhere a voice is calling,' and there is not a dry eye in the regiment."[10]

When the band rejoined Pershing a year later, this time as part of the American Expeditionary Force in France, the general made use of it for diplomatic purposes. The French city of Nice presented the band with a decorative banner "as a token of appreciation for their excellent music and the high esteem in which the organization is held by the people of Nice."[11]

Orville K. Wilson Sr., who organized the band in South Carolina, had served as an enlisted man through the band's Mexican deployment and was commissioned only after their recall to service with the Eighty-first Division. Even the band did not escape the human cost of the First World War: Wilson died in uniform in the war's immediate aftermath, in January of 1919, perishing of bronchial pneumonia. He did not survive to see the award of this commemorative banner.

371st Regiment

No, Sir; I'm not going "to France." I'm going "through France."
—A black conscript from a Southern state, quoted by W. Allison Sweeney[12]

More than two million black U.S. males between twenty-one and thirty-one registered for conscription. Even though this represented 10 percent of total draft registration, there were only four "Buffalo Soldier" regiments in the U.S. Army to take in these new soldiers, and none of those regiments was slated for AEF service. With some reluctance, the War Department agreed to create a new combat division in the national army for them.

The new Ninety-third would be this organization. Its first organized regiment started as the First Provisional Infantry Regiment (Colored), trained at Camp Jackson in Columbia. They would report late in 1917, the War Department having delayed the reporting date of these Southern recruits to prevent a projected labor shortage for the 1917 cotton harvest. Captain Chester Heywood, a company commander, found the initial appearance of his men uninspiring, but "clean clothes, well cooked food in quantity, systematic exercises and drill, regular hours, plus strict but intelligent discipline, soon worked wonders."[13] They trained as part of the white Eighty-first Division, but were reassigned to the Ninety-third before going to battle.

The regiment's white commander, Colonel Perry Miles, was a West Point graduate and a Distinguished Service Medal holder. Familiar with the Buffalo Soldiers from his previous service, Miles was confident of the potential of his new unit and determined to realize that potential. Nevertheless, training was a struggle.

Many of the officers assigned to the unit were initially dismayed, doubting the combat abilities of black soldiers, conscripts or both. Miles, meanwhile, had confidence in his troops but doubts about his inexperienced white junior officers. He assigned all of them to additional night classes in tactics and field operations, giving them less free time and eventually a higher esprit de corps than their fellows in other regiments. Soon the regiment's superior performance in training was noted.

Despite exceptional progress in military skills and discipline and all of the extracurricular studies required of its officers, the regiment narrowly missed reassignment as laborers by the War Department. Officers and men alike celebrated the avoidance of that ignominious fate when the regiment was officially designated the 371st Infantry and assigned to the new 93rd Division in December 1917.

Upon arrival in France, the Ninety-third Division's regiments shortly found themselves "on loan" to America's allies. Starved for replacements and long accustomed to employing African colonial troops, the French army eagerly took in the black American soldiers.

371st Infantry Regiment flag, hand painted on silk. *Courtesy South Carolina Confederate Relic Room and Military Museum.*

American commanding General "Black Jack" Pershing, whose nickname referred to his Buffalo Soldier service in the Spanish-American War, agreed to this arrangement, perhaps to help mollify the French demand for recruits. (Despite Pershing's own positive experiences with the Buffalo Soldiers, racial prejudice among white American soldiers contributed to the decision as well.)

Transfer to French command was a mixed experience for the troops. Colonel Hayward, commanding the 369th Regiment, wrote that "our great American general simply put the black orphan in a basket, set it on the doorstep of the French, pulled the bell and walked away. I said this to a French colonel...and he said 'weelcome leetle black babie.'"[14]

This pragmatic welcome was followed by some dismaying changes for the men, as they were required to turn in their Springfield rifles for the inferior French-issue Lebel and trade the rest of their United States Army accoutrements for their French equivalents. The troops would fight in American uniforms but with French equipment, even eating French rations, which would prove distinctly disappointing even though they initially included a daily liter of wine.

The 371st and its sister regiments of the 93rd Division fought through the remainder of the war under French command, earning Allied accolades for bravery in battle. In fact Pershing would later ask to have the now battle-tested regiments returned to the American Expeditionary Force, but the French, very pleased with their performance, did not agree. For their part the troops of the 93rd would demonstrate considerable

M1910 mess kit of Captain William W. Lewis, 105th Ammunition Train, 30th Division Artillery. *Courtesy South Carolina Confederate Relic Room and Military Museum.*

affection for the French army that had taken them in, and after the war they adopted a representation of their French helmets as the division's distinctive insignia.

After a seasoning period in a quiet sector, the soldiers of the 371st were ordered into the Meuse-Argonne offensive in September 1918. Serving well to the north of any other American troops, they advanced with the French against the German trench line and at last were engaged in fighting that would have a discernible influence on the outcome of the war.

"Hill 188" was the bitter Meuse-Argonne fight for which Corporal Freddie Stowers of the 371st's Company C was posthumously awarded a Congressional Medal of Honor. This fortified hill, protected by barbed wire and machine gun emplacements, was an important part of a German trench line. It was the objective of a 371st assault across "No Man's Land" on September 28, 1918. As the infantrymen advanced, a sham German surrender drew a large element of the 371st into the "kill zone" of a prepared ambush. When the attack was sprung, Stowers's company was nearly wiped out and its officers taken out of action. Corporal Stowers's leadership would then prove crucial to victory in this engagement as he took command, ignoring his own wounds to lead his fellow soldiers to close with and destroy a deadly machine gun position.

For the same fight, 371st Private Burton Holmes of Pendleton, South Carolina, a machine gunner, was posthumously awarded the Distinguished Service Cross for his heroism. South Carolina infantry soldiers of the black 371st, like their white counterparts in the 118th Regiment, suffered heavily during September and October of 1918, but this great final assault would finally bring the Great War to an end.

French gratitude to the 371st was expressed in General Order 265 from General Goybet's Headquarters:

> *The 157th DI will never forget the irresistible and heroic rush of the colored American regiments up the "Cote dis Observatoires" and into the "Plaine de Monthois." The most formidable defenses, the strongest machinegun nests, the most crushing artillery barrages were unable to stop them. These superior troops have overcome everything with a supreme disdain of death, and thanks to their courageous sacrifice, the Red (Bloody) Hand Division, for nine days of hard fighting always maintained the front rank in the 4th Army's victorious advance.*

Men of the 371st were awarded the French Legion of Honor, the Medaille Militaire and the Croix de Guerre with Bronze Palm. They would sail home in February of 1919 aboard the transport SS *Leviathan*.

Colonel Miles's farewell order thanked the men for "the uniform loyalty and faithfulness of your service and for the heroism and disregard of personal loss and suffering under the supreme test of battle." The city of Columbia would thank them as well, arranging "a community reception at Allen University in honor of their return of the 371st." The grand event was held on February 29, 1919. Community leaders, including I.S. Leevy and C.A. Johnson, spoke in honor of the regiment, and its two flags were presented to the community.

In the Trenches

United States troops arriving in France were immediately coveted by the other Allied powers, who wanted replacements for their own horrifying losses. General Pershing, following Woodrow Wilson's orders, would instead jealously guard the integrity of the American Expeditionary Force, insisting on its independent existence and national chain of command.

While their commander argued his case, the American soldiers were given British and French instructors for a final orientation to modern warfare and assigned to "quiet sectors" to gain experience. Here they experienced the reality of constant bombardment, suffered their first casualties and made their first forays into No Man's Land.

An infantryman of the 371st described duty in the static environment of the quiet sectors:

That Quiet Sector
Private Hilmar R. Baukhage, 371st Infantry, 1918

4 hours off—2 hours on—
And not a thing to do but think
And watch the mud and twisted wire
And never let your peepers blink.
Two hours on—4 hours off—
The dug-out's slimy as the trench;
It stinks of leather and stale smoke—
You wake up dopey from the stench.

Tedium and weariness might characterize service in a quiet sector, but the men also knew that even quiet sectors were not free of danger, and that in any case this period of seasoning would likely be followed by heavy combat. While the soldiers had the benefit of experienced instructors, they found themselves in a military environment vastly different from the battles the world's armies had trained for and expected, and they strove to master the new techniques and learn the unique hazards of the Western Front.

The fighting in France was characterized by great lines of fortification dug into the earth, where armies maneuvered in small spaces constricted by artillery and swept by machine gun fire. Thousands of lives might be expended for a gain of a few hundred yards of territory, a gain that was quite likely to be temporary, as the enemy regrouped in a further line of entrenchments to mount a counterattack.

The infantryman of the late nineteenth century had relied on his rifle and expected to march into battle, but in this environment the machine gun dominated long-range fighting and the line tactics of previous generations were suicidal. Trench raids, on the other hand, often devolved into pistol and hand grenade contests where a "trench sweeper" shotgun could prove superior to more conventional longarms. At any range,

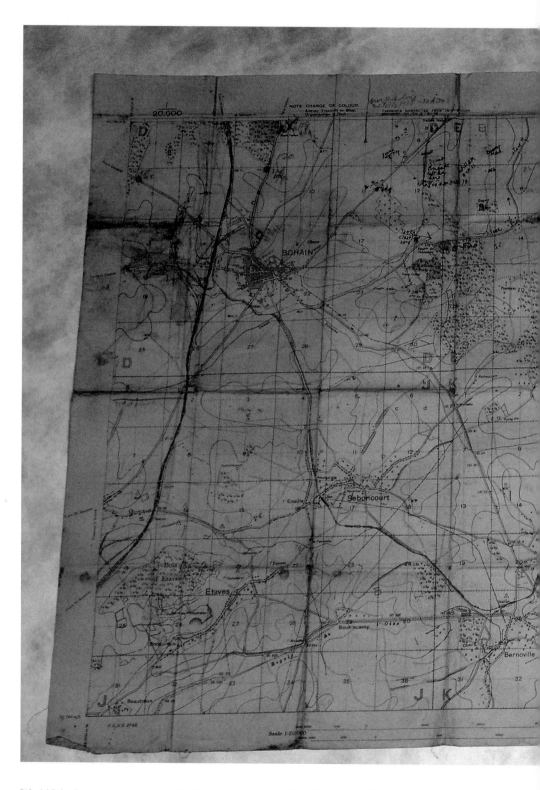

World War I trench map. *Courtesy South Carolina Confederate Relic Room and Military Museum.*

Western Front fighting was a brutal contest of attrition and had settled into a deadlock that the American Expeditionary Force would help to break.

Adding to the danger and misery was the constant danger of attack by poison gas. Gas warfare originated as an attempt to break the deadlock in the trenches, but soon became just another horrific feature of the front. First Sergeant Joseph Etheredge, who served in South Carolina's Field Hospital Number One (119th Field Hospital, 30th Division), graphically described the effects of a gas attack:

> *In being gassed by Mustard Gas, your throat commences burning as if you have taken a swallow of red-hot lead, your eyes commence burning and swelling shut as if a hive of bees had stung you, your voice goes from you till you can scarcely whisper, and you have a tremendous pressure on your chest as if there is a weight of from fifty to a hundred pounds there...It was about five weeks from the time I was gassed before I was able to turn over, and in fact it was about Armistice Day when I began to sit up a little.*[15]

Major Western Front battles for the South Carolina forces would include the St. Mihiel offensive, the Meuse-Argonne offensive and the Somme offensive, which, on September 29, 1918, broke the vaunted Hindenburg Line of German fortifications. The 118th Regiment would be the first unit to make a successful attack against that line. The long, bloody European stalemate was finally broken by the great fall campaign of 1918, and in that campaign, the American Expeditionary Force played its part as a cohesive army, just as Pershing (and President Wilson) had intended.

Aviation

The First World War would see the first large-scale use of aircraft for military purposes. Used at first for reconnaissance, they soon found other roles as well. As the use of aircraft proved advantageous, control of the skies was contested and the romanticized "Flying Aces" in their swift fighter planes attracted public notice. Meanwhile, the less glamorous reconnaissance flyers provided vital intelligence to the commanders on the ground, proving the worth of the airplane permanently. By the time American troops arrived in France, aircraft were a major component of strategy on both sides.

South Carolinians involved in aerial warfare included Major Harrison Saunders of Sumter, commanding the Twelfth Aero Squadron. Saunders's artillery experience proved critical as his reconnaissance squadron cooperated closely with Allied guns in support of the ground troops. South Carolinian Kiffin Rockwell served as a fighter pilot in French service in the famed Lafayette Escadrille, becoming the first American to shoot down an enemy plane in air combat—and dying in an air battle before the United States ever entered the war. Elliot White Springs and John Donaldson were two more prominent fighter pilots who called South Carolina home.

South Carolina's Shaw Air Force Base was named for First Lieutenant Ervin David Shaw, one of the first Americans to fly combat missions. Shaw, a Sumter County native,

M1918 field shoes of First Lieutenant George D. Levy, 323rd Infantry, 81st Division. *Courtesy South Carolina Confederate Relic Room and Military Museum.*

M1917 gas mask of Sergeant William H. Greene, Field Hospital 119, 105th Sanitary Train, 30th Division. *Courtesy South Carolina Confederate Relic Room and Military Museum.*

died after three enemy aircraft attacked his British-made Bristol F2B two-seater while he was returning from a reconnaissance mission.

Artillery

Although the machine gun is the weapon most associated with trench warfare in the popular conception, it was actually the massed artillery of the Western Front that caused the most casualties. The role of artillery in the First World War is difficult to overemphasize, both in its direct results and in the morale effect of continuous bombardment.

Sophisticated techniques were employed to isolate enemy units and prepare the ground for infantry advances, and the landscape of the battlefields was drastically

Field desk of Captain William W. Lewis, 105th Ammunition Train, 30th Division Artillery. *Courtesy South Carolina Confederate Relic Room and Military Museum.*

altered by the storms of high explosives unleashed by the big guns. The artillery also delivered the gas attacks, yet another innovation intended to break the bloody stalemate of static trench warfare.

Colonel William Wallace Lewis of York, South Carolina, served in the 105th Ammunition Train and in the 55th Field Artillery Brigade, part of the 30th Division. He described their stateside training: "That part of Camp Sevier allotted to the Artillery Brigade was a virgin forest, and many weeks were spent in clearing camp sites and drill grounds, but...the first general inspection of the Brigade showed that much progress was being made although the troops were being drilled on crude wooden imitation guns."[16]

Interior of field desk of Captain William W. Lewis, 105th Ammunition Train, 30th Division Artillery. *Courtesy South Carolina Confederate Relic Room and Military Museum.*

Despite this awkward beginning, the Thirtieth Division's artillerists would eventually master and employ French-pattern 75-millimeter guns, Schneider 155-millimeter howitzers and 3-inch Newton trench mortars in the battles of 1918. Supported by a mixture of mechanized and horse-drawn elements, they would be responsible for delivering the high-intensity bombardments critical to the success of Allied attacks.

Breakthrough!

Many Allied military planners anticipated the continuation of the Western Front stalemate well into 1919, and American troops began the war on the defensive as the German army attacked. However, the German army, weakened by four years of war, was more vulnerable than it appeared, and the American troops would soon provide critical assistance in bringing the long, bloody conflict to its conclusion.

The Allied "Hundred Days Offensive" in the autumn of 1918 finally collapsed an important section of the German defenses, and South Carolina's soldiers were in the forefront with a historic assault on the Hindenburg Line. This hundred-mile-long trench system across northeastern France was fortified with concrete bunkers, barbed wire, minefields, interlocking machine gun positions and tunnels that allowed German reinforcements to move to threatened sections in relative safety. German Generals Hindenburg and Ludendorf had great confidence in this supposedly impregnable position. Improved technology and fresh troops, however, would overwhelm the German army at last. In an attack that lasted from September 18 to October 5, 1918, British, Australian and American forces broke through and cleared the entire Hindenburg Line. With its defenses fatally breached, Germany acknowledged defeat, and the war ended with the signing of the armistice a month later.

South Carolina soldiers were in the forefront of this historic assault. Soldiers of the 30th Division, including the 118th Infantry Regiment, won particular praise for their part in the battle.

The Congressional Medal of Honor is the highest decoration for valor given to United States military personnel. Prior to the First World War, the standards for the medal had been vague, but a panel of officers was appointed in 1916 to review previous awards and establish that the honor be awarded only for "distinguished conduct by an officer or enlisted man in action involving actual conflict with an enemy."

In its attack on the Hindenburg Line and the campaign that followed, the 118th Infantry Regiment would win an astonishing six Congressional Medals of Honor, every one earned by a South Carolinian. Lieutenant James Dozier, Sergeant Gary Foster, Sergeant Thomas Hall, Sergeant Richard Hilton, Corporal John Villepegue and Corporal James Heriot were each awarded the nation's highest decoration for bravery for their actions in October of 1918. Both Heriot and Hall received their medals posthumously.

The citation of James Heriot reveals the character of the fighting in which these infantry soldiers were engaged. It reads, in part,

Cpl. Heriot, with 4 other soldiers, organized a combat group and attacked an enemy machine-gun nest which had been inflicting heavy casualties on his company. In the advance 2 of his men were killed, and because of the heavy fire from all sides the remaining 2 sought shelter. Unmindful of the hazard attached to his mission, Cpl. Heriot, with fixed bayonet, alone charged the machinegun, making his way through the fire for a distance of 30 yards and forcing the enemy to surrender.

Eighty-first Division newspaper dated May 17, 1919. *Courtesy South Carolina Confederate Relic Room and Military Museum.*

James Dozier, later the adjutant general of South Carolina for more than thirty years, earned his Congressional Medal of Honor as a first lieutenant. Dozier was South Carolina's most decorated soldier.

In command of 2 platoons, 1st Lt. Dozier was painfully wounded in the shoulder early in the attack, but he continued to lead his men, displaying the highest bravery and skill. When his command was held up by heavy machinegun fire, he disposed his men in the best cover available and with a soldier continued forward to attack a machinegun nest. Creeping up to the position in the face of intense fire, he killed the entire crew with hand grenades and his pistol and a little later captured a number of Germans who had taken refuge in a dugout nearby.

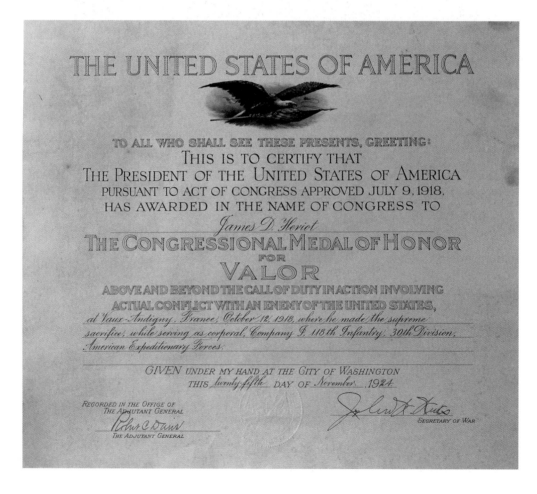

Medal of Honor certificate of Corporal James D. Heriot, 118th Infantry, 30th Division. *Courtesy South Carolina Confederate Relic Room and Military Museum.*

Medal of Honor of Corporal James D. Heriot, 118th Infantry, 30th Division. *Courtesy South Carolina Confederate Relic Room and Military Museum.*

The astonishing accomplishments of the 118th Regiment during the autumn of 1918 would reflect great credit on South Carolina's soldiers and contribute to hastening the armistice that brought Allied victory. Adjutant General Moore summarized the soldiers' record: "Their action under fire portrays an exhibition of the highest type of courage, bravery and heroism, which was excelled by none and equaled by few."[17]

Also recommended for the nation's highest military award was Corporal Freddie Stowers of the segregated 371st Infantry, who was killed in battle in September of 1918. Stowers's heroism was unquestioned, but his commander's recommendation for the award of the Congressional Medal of Honor was lost during the war's aftermath. Members of his family would finally accept his posthumous award in 1988 from President George Bush.

In the assault on Hill 188, a critical German defensive position, Stowers provided crucial leadership after his company's officers had all been incapacitated. From his citation:

> *Corporal Stowers took charge, setting such a courageous example of personal bravery and leadership that he inspired his men to follow him in the attack. With extraordinary heroism and complete disregard of personal danger under devastating fire, he crawled forward leading his squad toward an enemy machine gun nest, which was causing heavy casualties to his company. After fierce fighting, the machine gun position was destroyed and the enemy soldiers were killed. Displaying great courage and intrepidity, Corporal Stowers continued to press the attack against a determined enemy. While crawling forward and urging his men to continue the attack on a second trench line, he was gravely wounded by machine gun fire. Although, Corporal Stowers was mortally wounded, he pressed forward, urging on the members of his squad, until he died. Inspired by the heroism and display of bravery of Corporal Stowers, his company continued the attack against incredible odds, contributing to the capture of Hill 188 and causing heavy enemy casualties.*

The heroism of the men of the 118th, 371st and South Carolina's other battlefield units helped drive the final advance that forced an armistice and an end to the First World War. South Carolina's Adjutant General Moore expressed a common hope in his annual report for 1918 when he said that the year "in all human probability will go down into future history as the culmination of the world's greatest war."[18] Certificates issued by President Woodrow Wilson would acclaim America's "Great War" soldiers as "The Chivalry of a New Humanity," and the surviving soldiers returned to their homes with hopes for a lasting peace.

A CALL FOR ALL:
THE GREAT WAR SUMMONS THE PALMETTO STATE

Jason Shaiman, McKissick Museum,
University of South Carolina

In the Palmetto State, like elsewhere in the country, the call for all to support the United States' interest in the war began before April 6, 1917. In the few days before Wilson declared war on Germany, Americans knew that the United States' entry in the war was inevitable. Wilson had long advocated neutrality, yet the American media sensationalized the war, influenced by propaganda steadily streaming from Britain, France and Belgium. The methods for distributing the propaganda utilized by the United States government were diverse and included newspapers, music, posters, advertisements, film and educational materials. Such a wide range of propaganda allowed the government's position in the war effort to infiltrate the consciousness of all Americans. South Carolina, like other states, was not immune to the steady stream of messages issued by the government and used to raise the financial and military support needed to enter what would become the Great War. An examination of the government's propaganda methods reveals the patterns and trends of dissemination used in the Palmetto State, and places the local efforts within a national perspective.

Americans' first encounter with propaganda for World War I came in the form of newspapers. At first, the public was repulsed by the war, seeing the conflict as seemingly senseless, unnecessary and unjustified. One Dutch Fork, South Carolina farmer expressed his opinion that a few lives would surely be lost in the war in Europe, but that many more would be lost if the United States entered the war.[1] Even after twenty months of fighting, beginning in 1914, between British and German forces the general sentiment was "the desire of the great majority of the American people to avoid war, so long as it...[could] possibly be avoided."[2] However, once British propaganda made its way into mainstream American newspapers, attitudes began to change and Americans became interested in the fight. It was hard not to feel sympathy for the plights of the British, French and Belgians as represented in the newspapers.

The continued dominance of newspapers in the formulation of public opinion was largely because radio was still in its infancy and was not yet utilized for civilian or

The Columbia Record

THE LARGEST AFTERNOON DAILY IN THE CAROLINAS

STATE OF WAR IS DECLARED
All Interned German Ships Are Seized

"STATE OF WAR IS DECLARED." *Columbia Record*, April 8, 1917.

Above: "The Harvest Fields of Death," *Leslie's Illustrated Weekly Newspaper*, November 18, 1915. *Courtesy of the South Carolina Confederate Relic Room and Military Museum. Robert L. Brown Collection*

Opposite: Crédit Commercial de France. 4éme Emprunt de la Defense Nationale. Souscrivez pour la victoire et pour triomph…de la Liberté. Lucien Jonas, 1880–1947, lithograph on paper, 1918. Joseph M. Bruccoli Great War Collection, Thomas Cooper Library, University of South Carolina

Above: *Keep these of the U.S.A.: Buy more Liberty Bonds*, John Norton, lithograph on paper, 1917–18. *Courtesy Joseph M. Bruccoli Great War Collection, Thomas Cooper Library, University of South Carolina.*

Opposite: *Clear the Way!!* Howard Chandler Christy, lithograph on paper, 1917–18. *Courtesy Joseph M. Bruccoli Great War Collection, Thomas Cooper Library, University of South Carolina.*

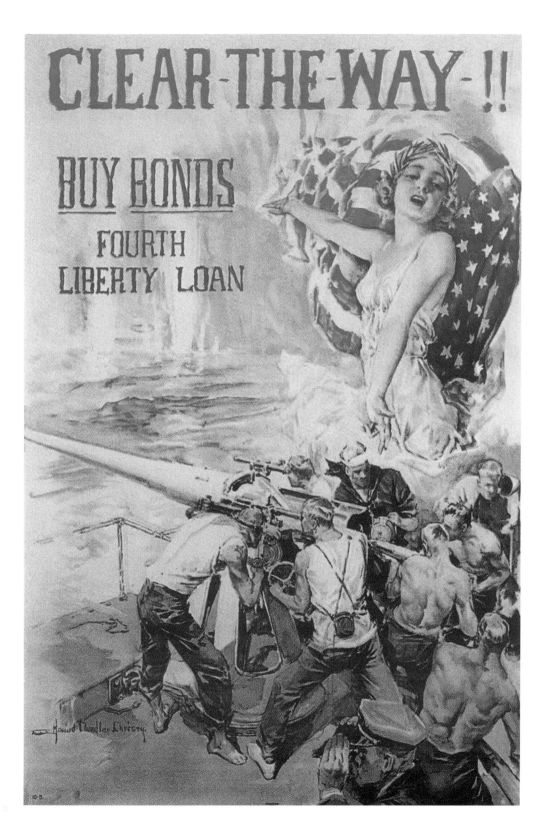

military communications. After the United States declared war on Germany, General John J. Pershing, commander of the United States Armies, advocated the need for a radio system to assist with military operations on the Western Front, as well as a means of promoting the progress of the war back home. However, the technology was not made readily available until 1920 and without the use of radio as a major means of communication and dissemination of information, the government had to rely on other means of promoting the war.

By World War I, newspapers had long been utilized to inflame public passions. From the American Revolution and through the Civil War, South Carolinians, like many other Americans, received much of their information and formed many of their opinions based on news publications and broadsides. However, in the United States, "it was customary during the years of neutrality to consider American opinion on geographical lines. In so far as newspapers were concerned, critics were unanimous in differentiating between the Atlantic seaboard attitude and that of the Middle and Far West. The South as a unit was usually ignored."[3] New York was seen by the British as the most important destination for the distribution of war reports to the American people. The *New York Times* was recognized as a pro-Ally (primarily British) paper, while the *Tribune* (New York) was considered pro-French. Many of the editors of the big New York papers felt that news organizations such as the *World*, the second largest newspaper in New York, was "the mouthpiece of the Administration" (U.S. government). The large papers were vigorously pro-Ally to the extent that they shunned any paper that did not take a similar stance. Papers that did not present sympathetic tones toward the Allies were often considered pro-German.[4] In a poll taken by the *Literary Digest* on November 14, 1914, reflecting partisan feelings of editors, forty-seven out of fifty-two Southern editors were pro-Ally. The poll also showed that of 103 Southern cities, 71 were pro-Ally, 28 were neutral and 4 were considered pro-German.[5]

Although the South was still considered to be of little importance regarding political opinions following the aftermath of the Civil War, Southerners of every race and religion were in fact eager to know where the United States stood regarding the war. Southern newspapers such as the *Columbia Record* (Columbia) and the *News and Courier* (Charleston) were vigilant about presenting quality and up-to-date information, albeit propaganda, about the war to their respective communities. Much of this information came from the federal and state government, as well as activities taking place in local communities. South Carolinians learned a great deal through larger papers, such as the *News and Courier*, *Columbia Record* and the *Greenville Times*, as well as smaller papers including the *Sumter Item*, *Aiken Standard* and the *Greenwood Index Journal*. Prior to and after the declaration of war, South Carolina papers covered the news of the war overseas and mentioned many of the local war efforts including parades, meetings, sermons, fundraisers and other events. Headlines also reported major events, including the April 2, 1914 *Columbia Record* headline "President will make his Address Tonight—Wilson speaks at 8 o'clock."[6]

It is important to remember, however, that newspaper organizations often printed biased views of the war. Albert J. Beveridge, a senator from Indiana, expressed his concerns with this problem when he commented, "I fear the American people know very little of what is going on."[7] The assessment of papers across the country showed that most of the commentary and reports of the war were printed in the editorials, a section rarely read by many Americans. Strategically placed, many of the larger papers using this tactic attempted to reach a specific group of readers—affluent, highly literate white men. This, in turn, had the important economic and political effect desired by the papers, as the wealthy made the most influential financial and philosophical contributions to the war effort. This reaching out to the wealthy and more influential segment of South Carolina's population negated the opportunity for most of the state's citizens to voice their opinions in a manner that would have any impact on how the war would affect the Palmetto State and the nation.

Unlike most of the large national papers, the *Columbia Record* and the *News and Courier* printed a great deal of material on the front page of their papers. These papers used a top-down approach in providing international news on the front page and progressing to local news by the last page. Editors of the most prominent South Carolina newspapers understood that the international scene in relation to America was important and that Carolinians needed to understand the government's stance on the war. American sympathy for Britain, France and Belgium increased as headlines illustrated the horrors inflicted upon those nations. Women and children became increasingly sympathetic to the cause after hearing of the deaths of innocent American citizens traveling on steam liners sunk by German U-boats in the Atlantic Ocean from England to America. The accounting of what occurred on a local level was the responsibility of regional papers throughout the state, and each day the news hit closer to home. Reports of German attacks on U.S. merchant ships struck a chord with Americans and hit hard with businessmen whose investments in cargo and the shipping industry were heavily impaired. It was the sinking of the *Lusitania* that finally brought about a common opinion of the war and anti-German sentiments. Americans on the East Coast, especially in New York, were at the helm of those advocating a declaration of war on Germany.[8]

Shortly after the declaration of war on April 6, 1917, a presidential executive order established the Committee on Public Information (CPI) for the purpose of issuing propaganda to the American people and rallying the American people behind the country's war effort through all methods of service, from industrial to agricultural and from education to media. Up to this point, Americans' exposure to propaganda mainly involved newspapers; however, the creation of CPI changed the format of propaganda dramatically and citizens were soon barraged with military messages through numerous approaches.

The Wilson administration kept tight control on the information newspapers presented to the American people. In order to maintain a consistent tone and message throughout the country, the CPI was the clearinghouse for all war correspondence and public information printed in newspapers and journals in the United States. They also monitored all materials circulating in the United States from organizations in Europe as well as information sent from the United States overseas. The first was an attempt to prevent any pro-German sentiments from infiltrating the United States, while the latter was to prevent sensitive information from reaching enemy hands.

To further control the media, the president hired George Creel to head the CPI. Creel, the publisher of the *Kansas City Independent* and editor of *Rocky Mountain News*, was an outspoken supporter of Wilson. Rather than relying solely on newspapers, Creel concentrated on publishing pamphlets. The most popular pamphlets distributed were "Loyalty Leaflets" and two series of pamphlets titled "Red, White and Blue Series" and the "War Information Series." These were simple appeals to workingmen to support the war and were not targeted to any specific region, but to all Americans. Between 1917 and 1918 millions of leaflets and pamphlets were distributed to newspapers, chambers of commerce, manufacturers' associations, labor unions, banks, general stores, YMCA branches, post offices, railroad stations, state councils on defense and nearly ten thousand public libraries.[9]

The CPI also established the *Official Bulletin*, America's first government publication. The paper ran daily, except Sundays, from May 1917 through March 1919. Circulation of this paper reached a high of 115,031 subscriptions by October 1918. A copy of the *Official Bulletin* was sent to nearly every military camp across the country as well as to some 54,000 post offices.[10] The *Official Bulletin* contained all pronouncements, statements, executive orders and proclamations issued by the president since the declaration of war. It listed almost every casualty released by the American Army and Navy, as well as the names of prisoners of war, wounded soldiers and those cited for bravery. The *Official Bulletin* essentially was a means of communicating to the people the daily affairs of government officials in Washington pertaining to the war. It also served as a means of distributing news to newspaper and magazine organizations across the country and controlling what the government wanted them to print and promote.

Under Creel's direction the CPI created two divisions that targeted the non-reading populace: the Division of Pictorial Publicity, established in April 1917, and the Division of Advertising, established in January 1918. The Division of Advertising was established "for the purpose of receiving and directing through the proper channels the generous offers of advertising forces of the nation" in the effort to "inform public opinion properly and adequately."[11] However, the most vivid means of propaganda were posters, which fell under the Division of Pictorial Publicity. Many artists were recruited by the War Department to create propaganda posters and other works promoting widespread support of the war effort. Between 1917 and 1918 thousands of posters and other propaganda materials were created and disseminated across the country. The most prominent works were the posters, which today are highly collected works of military propaganda as well as works of art in their own right.

The Division of Pictorial Publicity was under the direction of Charles Dana Gibson, the most influential and best-known magazine illustrator in America at the time. A self-organized group of artists and illustrators in the division, known as the Vigilantes, included Charles Dana Gibson, Jack Sheridan, C.B. Falls, Howard Chandler Christy and James Montgomery Flagg (best known for creating the iconic image of Uncle

Boys and Girls! You can Help your Uncle Sam Win the War, James Montgomery Flagg, lithograph on paper, 1917–18. *Courtesy War Savings Stamps.*

Sam).[12] The Division of Advertising created the ideas and concepts, yet it was up to Gibson and the other Vigilantes to create the imagery behind the message.

Like many others, Gibson felt that because of geographic distance America was too removed from the war in a physical and psychological sense to truly grasp its impact and larger implications. He felt that until Americans really felt the horror of the war, they would not be emotionally involved in the war effort. In 1918 Gibson stated that "the spirit that will lead a man to put away the things of his accustomed life and go forth to all the hardships of war is not kindled by showing him the facts."[13] He felt that the war must appeal to the heart of all Americans. For this reason, many illustrations used in the posters commonly posted throughout cities and towns included expressionist qualities intended to strike at the heart through color and provocative content. None of the posters issued by the CPI were directed at any specific states, including South Carolina, but were printed in mass quantities and distributed throughout the nation, circulating the same message to all Americans.

Some posters and illustrations were intended to reach out to specific groups of people, whether in the workplace or in the home. C.T. Adams, an artist and illustrator, created a series of images encouraging men to enlist as shipyard workers. These posters, titled U.S. Shipyard Volunteers, were instrumental in recruiting the thousands of skilled workers necessary to build the new fleet of merchant and naval vessels needed in the war. Posters like these encouraged men to enlist in support of the war working at the Charleston Navy Yard. Artist Hubert L. Towle from Philadelphia created posters supporting labor and directed toward workers as well as employers. Posters reaching out to the labor force often featured campaigns such as "The Right Men in the Right Jobs Will Win the War." Other posters reached out to women and children, illustrating what they could do to support the war in which their husbands and fathers were fighting. Several posters targeted women by encouraging them to write letters to their loved ones fighting in Europe. Others suggested that women get involved in food drives and food conservation and join the Red Cross.

Creel also gave significant attention to obtaining the help of libraries across the country to disseminate propaganda to the people. At first, libraries, as well as many other community-based institutions, maintained a status of neutrality in regard to the war. However, almost immediately after war was declared, Walter Brown, president of the American Libraries Association, wrote to Creel asking whether "you were interested in what the library might do in the way of publicity in connection with the work of your Bureau."[14] Librarians soon requested that the Committee on Public Information place libraries on mailing lists to receive important war reports and propaganda: "The public libraries, by furnishing their readers with the best books, pamphlets, maps, and magazines, domestic and foreign, by displaying them on open shelves, by printing lists of the most important books and articles, by holding exhibitions of war materials, may likewise help to make the war a personal challenge and a definite and familiar task to the general public."[15] Others supported the notion that the public library should "act as an agency of patriotic publicity, and post and distribute any government war literature."[16] This included all aspects of propaganda, such as the president's messages and war

Books Wanted, C.B. Falls, lithograph on paper, 1917–18. *Courtesy Joseph M. Bruccoli Great War Collection, Thomas Cooper Library, University of South Carolina.*

proclamations, state decrees concerning war emanating from the governor's office, any bulletins distributed by federal and state departments and any information circulated by the Red Cross or other voluntary associations.

Alice Jordan of the Boston Public Library stressed that children needed to understand the reasons for the current conflict in which the United States had entered when she stated that the war was "a great opportunity to the worker with children to stimulate an interest in history and to arouse and quicken a true sense of patriotism."[17] This became a national trend for libraries that attempted to gain the attention of children and inspire them to learn about American and European history.

Propaganda controlled by the CPI was also distributed to the schools and was intended to reach teachers and students. Many teachers complained that they received too much information and that they did not have time to cull through all the materials and present them to their students. To address this issue, a central system was created with the National School Service bulletin, first published in January 1919.[18] The intent of the materials was to create stronger support of the United States and its involvement in the war. Their hopes were also to attract the attention of the parents. The sixteen-page National School Service paper was issued twice a month and distributed directly to schools, not the superintendents. Circumventing the superintendents was an effort to put the information directly into the hands of the teachers, not to be censored by state superintendents and "to keep up the proper patriotic morale behind the lines" by making "every school pupil a messenger for Uncle Sam."[19] The National School Service took special interest in rural America, including many areas of South Carolina. More than half of the schoolchildren in America were believed to attend rural or village schools. Teachers were poorly prepared and had little money to provide for the students, and illiteracy was high. The intent was to draw rural America into a larger spectrum and involve it in national issues.

News was also distributed in the form of pictures and film. The Film Division of the Committee on Public Information was created in late 1917. Newsreels were produced and played in movie houses throughout the country. Columbia, the capital of South Carolina, had at least three movie houses, including the Ideal Theater located on Main Street, the heart of the downtown leading directly to the statehouse. Greenville, located in the Upstate, had at least two theaters in the downtown area, while the historic port city of Charleston included at least three movie houses. Originally the Film Division distributed U.S. Army Signal Corps movies. The signal corps, founded in 1860, was formed to develop and test communication equipment for the battlefield. The corps also created films, including *Under Four Flags* and *America's Answer* in 1918. Ironically, *Under Four Flags* was released six days following the armistice. D.W. Griffith, a contributor to the Film Division, attempted to reform the motion picture industry, believing that movies could be used to create a sense of universal ethics and integrity.

Since radio was unavailable for the distribution of military information and the spread of nationalistic sentiments during World War I, music was used to create a patriotic atmosphere with live performances. World War I inspired many great composers and songwriters to symbolize the American spirit in music. Songs were about family back home and, more

Great War Film: Our American Boys in the European War, Victor Tardieu, lithograph on paper, 1917–18. *Courtesy American Ambulance Field Service.*

"Oh! How I Hate to Get Up in the Morning." Sheet music for hit song from *Yip-Yip-Yaphank*, written by Irving Berlin. Published by Waterson, Berlin, and Snyder, New York, 1918. *Joseph M. Bruccoli Great*

importantly, sweethearts and spouses. Music written by composers such as Irving Berlin, Ernest R. Ball, Billy Baskette and George M. Cohan captured the essence of the emotions that ran deep through the hearts of many soldiers and loved ones. Other songs like Berlin's "Good-Bye France (You'll Never Be Forgotten by the U.S.A.)" helped establish a rapport with the Allied nations, while "Farewell, Mother I Hate to Say Good-bye to You" and other songs touched the hearts of many as the reality of the war effort in America took its toll on families. Berlin's famous "Oh! How I Hate to Get Up in the Morning" took a lighthearted approach to illustrating life in the military and the difficulties for new enlistees in adjusting to a new life.

A large number of these patriotic songs were available in recordings for playing in the home. Additionally, song sheets with lyrics were available, further promoting the personal connections with the war effort. These song sheets could be purchased at many music stores throughout South Carolina, especially in larger cities such as Columbia and Charleston. Song sheet covers utilized visuals created by many of the great illustrators of the time. The song sheet cover for "Farewell, Mother I Hate to Say Good-bye to You" shows a soldier bidding farewell to his mother outside their pastoral home. In the front yard is a flag with two stars, illustrating that two members of her family were fighting in the war. Other song sheet covers, such as "Bring Me a Letter from My Old Home Town," illustrate a family writing letters to son and brother, Sergeant Winslow Brown, serving in France.

As radio was unknown to most of the world, music at the time was mostly enjoyed in the home or at public events such as dances and concerts. In the 1920s and 1930s, a time when radio was the new voice box for the country, Jim Whitaker hosted a show on WCSC in Charleston called *Whitaker's Wax Works*. This radio show aired many songs written in 1917 and 1918 specifically for the Great War. Whitaker added these old hits to his selections in the 1960s when the staff at Fort McPherson, Georgia, offered him radio time promoting the recruitment of army reserve units.

The patriotic songs written during 1917 and 1918 were also featured in many parades and civic events, such as Civic Preparedness Days and Liberty Bond and war stamp drives. In Charleston, a concert by Metz's Military Band was held at Hampton Park on April 8, 1917, promoting American patriotism. Similar concerts were held in Greenville, Columbia, Greenwood and Florence, drawing tens of thousands of South Carolinians.

Several patriotic events were held throughout the state in the days prior to the announcement of the United States' entry into the war. On March 25, 1917, the city of Greenville hosted a parade that drew fifteen thousand people. The city held another event on March 30, which was recognized as the first War Preparedness Parade in South Carolina. The parade drew a crowd of nearly twenty thousand people, including students, children, Confederate veterans and the local Red Cross chapter.

The April 3 edition of the *Columbia Record* announced a rally in Columbia to be held on April 5, with the headline "Celebration of Entry into War Will Likely Draw Thousands—All Elements Unite for Big Rally." In order to ensure that this would be the biggest rally and parade in the state, a circular was sent out to thousands of Columbians calling them to participate and to show their patriotism in the state's capital. The circular

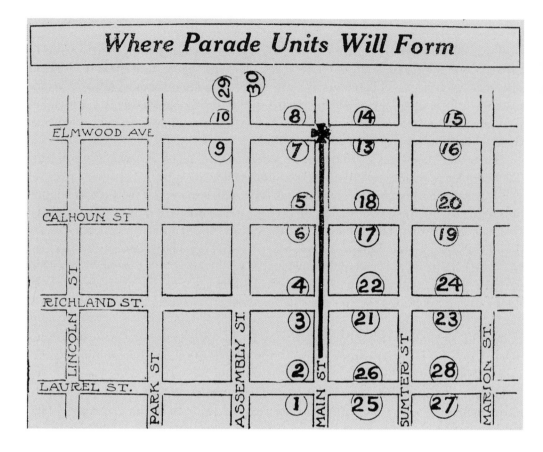

"Where Parade Units Will Form" (Columbia Civic Preparedness Day Parade Map). *Columbia Record*, April 4, 1917.

stated, "Now is the time for Columbians to let it be known in no uncertain terms that they stand squarely behind the nation and President Wilson in this emergency." The parade began at Elmwood Avenue and traveled down Main Street up to the steps of the capitol. A number of military and civic groups participated in the rally. The April 5 article quoted Joe Sparks, chair of the Preparedness Day Celebration Committee, as stating:

> *All fraternal organizations, civic bodies, camps of veterans, college students, school children, labor unions, women's service units and other organizations of Columbia are urged to join in the preparedness parade. In further preparation for the parade the Columbia chapter of the Red Cross formally organized the night before the parade and marched demonstratively with other groups in Columbia. Included in the day's festivities were the United Confederate Veterans, Boy Scouts, Mill band and employees of Pacific Mills, Columbia Fire Department, Knights of Columbus, Plumbers Union No. 227, Red Cross, and the Y.M.C.A.*[20]

It was estimated that over fifteen thousand people participated in the parade. The principal speaker for the rally was to be former Governor John C. Sheppard. However, due to Sheppard's extended illness, Robert G. Rhett, former mayor of Charleston and president of the chamber of commerce, spoke for Sheppard. Although a last-minute change in the program, Rhett's presence further illustrates the united effort made by South Carolinians to support President Wilson.[21]

"Thousand March Under 'Old Glory'" was a headline in the *News and Courier* on April 13, 1917. An estimated eight thousand people attended a parade in Florence where "the whole town was decorated with bunting and flags and from every store place of business and residence the Stars and Stripes, 'Old Glory,' was displayed and on many buildings by its side floated the Stars and Bars of the Confederacy, as beloved Palmetto flag."[22] The Confederacy and the War Between the States were still in the consciousness of many South Carolinians, especially veterans. Many South Carolinians drew references between the Great War and the Civil War as fights for political and social freedoms. In addition, an opportunity for Southerners to demonstrate their military strength offered a great sense of pride.

In cities and towns across the Atlantic seaboard, especially those that had taken up arms during the Civil War, speeches were written to target certain ideals and historical events. The vocal strength of Americans promoting the war also took place on the streets through public speaking, one of the most rousing and direct means of propaganda, and a method of which the CPI took full advantage. In order to reach out to the non-reading section of the populace the CPI organized a national speakers' network, based on a group of speakers established in Chicago called the Four Minute Men. Curtis Nicholson, the coordinator for the Southern circuit of Four Minute Men, was given the task of recruiting speakers and directed the distribution of speeches throughout cities, towns and rural communities.[23]

In public squares, movie houses and theaters, the Four Minute Men, as they became known based on the length of their impromptu speeches, supported the war by reaching out to the masses. These speeches also served as a means of informing communities, towns and cities about state activities in the war and what actions were being taken by the government. Although the Four Minute Men began by speaking about the Chamberlain Bill, a call for universal military training, they found themselves speaking about the need for greater support in the war effort.[24] Their speeches were made to appeal and to inspire, not to inflame and create fervent hatred. Highly successful, Four Minute Men groups spread throughout the country with numbers rising from 2,500 in July 1917 to 15,000 in November. By the end of 1918, there were nearly 75,000 speakers making nearly one million speeches to a gross audience of almost 400 million people.

Four Minute Men organizations proved to be highly successful for three primary reasons. First, they employed volunteers to speak to their local communities, both in cities such as Columbia and Charleston and in smaller towns such as Florence and Aiken. This allowed for the most effective utilization of resources and knowledge of locations in which to make speeches. Second, they took advantage of ready-made audiences (places where crowds naturally congregated) such as movie houses, theaters, markets and town squares. Finally, control from the national headquarters in Washington, D.C., dictated the exact speeches. Across the country the same four-minute topics were being addressed so that continuity of agenda was controlled.

One of the speeches made October 1917 reads:

> *Ladies and Gentlemen:*
>
> *I have just received the information that there is German spy among us—A German spy watching us.*
>
> *He is around here somewhere, reporting upon you and me—sending reports about us to Berlin and telling the Germans just what we are doing with the Liberty Loan. From every section of the country these spies have been getting reports over to Potsdam—not general reports but details—where the loan is going well and where its success seems weak, and what people are saying in each community.*
>
> *For the German Government is worried about our great loan. Those Junkers fear its effect upon the German morale. They're raising a loan this month, too.*
>
> *If the American people lend their billions now, one and all with a hip-hip-hurrah, it means that America is united and strong. While if we lend our money half-heartedly, America seems weak and autocracy remains strong.*
>
> *Money means everything now; it means quicker victory and therefore less bloodshed. We are in the war, and now Americans can have but one option, only one wish in the Liberty Loan.*
>
> *Well, I hope these spies are getting their messages straight, letting Potsdam know that America is hurling back to the autocrats these answers:*
>
> *For treachery here, attempted treachery in Mexico, treachery everywhere—one billion.*
>
> *For murder of American women and children—one billion more.*
>
> *For broken faith and promise to murder more Americans—billions and billions more. And then we will add:*
>
> *In the world fight for Liberty, our share—billions and billions and billions and endless billions.*
>
> *Do not let the German spy hear and report that you are a slacker.*[25]

Women were often found making Four Minute speeches. Those included were Ida Tarbell and Jane Addams, both in Chicago. Tarbell spoke on behalf of the Woman's Committee on the Council of National Defense, while Addams spoke on behalf of the Food Administration.[26]

The Division of Women's War Work, founded in November 1917, sought to mobilize women, with materials from the division being sent to almost twenty thousand newspapers and women's publications. The division served two main functions: it sent letters to women who raised questions concerning the war and it produced feature articles and news stories about the work of women. These stories illustrated the impact of women at home and abroad and what they accomplished through national organizations, government employment, state and local organizations, schools, colleges and churches.

A large number of posters and pamphlets targeted women asking them what they could do to help their boys on the Western Front, while other posters attempted to recruit women to serve as nurses overseas and to help their country in every capacity on the homefront. Features also noted the work of African American women.

In a newspaper article printed on April 8, 1917, the African American women of Columbia planned to meet and join together in support of the war. A statement on behalf of the women organizing the meeting noted,

> *The colored women of this city and state being deeply imbued with the spirit of patriotism and loyalty to their State and country at this time, when our great nation is at war with a very formidable foe, feel it necessary and deem it fitting and proper as patriotic daughters of South Carolina, to put ourselves on record now as being willing and ready to protect our country's best interest by organizing now our service, when our country calls, and call it must and will when the crucial moment is at hand. We are prepared by education, training and sympathy to render the same kind of service that any other woman will render and we, as our forefathers, Carney Chrispus Attucks and others, will see to it that "Old Glory, our dear old flag," will never touch the ground.* [27]

Four Minute Men speeches attempted to appeal to African Americans to win their support. Following Liberia's declaration of war on Germany because the Kaiser favored slavery and felt that Africans had no place in Germany, the U.S. government wanted African American citizens to also support the war against Germany. [28] Sentiments like these were targeting specific ethnic groups to draw out not only their American patriotism, but also their pride of heritage.

African Americans from South Carolina made a significant effort to establish a regiment of soldiers, further illustrating the notion of "support from all classes." The U.S. Army provided enlistment opportunities to blacks, for which more than a thousand earned officers' commissions. Ray Nelson, a well-known African American from Columbia, announced that he was taking steps "to raise a regiment of negroes who would give their service to the United States at the call of the President." [29] However, in South Carolina these opportunities were delayed compared to some areas of the nation. Governor Manning was reluctant to let such a regiment be formed, as he felt that their service was better needed here in South Carolina working toward food production and conservation. Another issue taking African Americans out of South Carolina was Northern labor agents, who were trying to entice African Americans from South Carolina to go to the North. Governor Manning began offering rewards for the apprehension of these labor agents as the governor felt that African Americans were being lured unfaithfully.

Patriotic speeches were also made to university students in South Carolina to encourage enlistment in the military. Colonel Henry T. Thompson of Columbia gave a short address to the student body at the University of South Carolina. Thompson spoke of "military training and the necessity for a national system of training for defense." [30] Knowing the history of USC students taking up arms, as proved during the Civil

Joan of Arc Saved France, Haskell Coffin, lithograph on paper, 1917–18. *Courtesy War Savings Stamps.*

War, Thompson knew that his appeal to the student body would produce a significant number of enlisted men if the need arose. In fact, by April 4, 203 students and 11 professors had enrolled in a class teaching military training.[31] Understanding that there was great hesitation among Americans in regard to entering the war, he referred to the student body a speech made by John Grier Hibben, president of Princeton University. A professed pacifist, Hibben spoke of his personal ideals, but knowing that if war was inevitable he needed to support his country.[32] Ironically, Hibben had succeeded Woodrow Wilson as the president of Princeton University.

Many speeches were given at the height of the Liberty Bond and Victory Loan Drives throughout the United States and proved to be very successful. Three Liberty Loan Drives and one Victory Loan Drive were organized on a national level to give financial support to the war. Purchasing bonds provided a way for people to invest money in the war and to receive benefits in the form of financial returns on their investments. The wealthy were persuaded to support a cause by investing their money. The Homestead Bank in Columbia promoted the sales of war bonds in the newspaper with ads explaining how to purchase bonds.

Several banks throughout the state promoted their financial offerings to the public through newspaper ads prior to the declaration of war. However, when the fund drive known as the Liberty Loan of 1917 began in May 1917, banks took every opportunity to show their patriotic duty as well as improve their financial status within the world of lending institutions. Subscriptions for bonds were typically offered in $50, $100 and $200 increments. Several banks such as the Germania National Bank in Charleston offered periodic payment plans with small deposits toward the purchase of bonds. Charleston banks were the most prolific in advertising the sale of bonds, some purchasing half-page ads in the *News and Courier*. Full-page ads for the sale of Liberty Loans were also printed as a national message of encouraging support. Women and children were often targeted for the purchasing of subscriptions. Messages expressed the idea that loose change and spare money could be used to purchase war bonds to help America win the war.[33]

The Bank of Sumter printed a pamphlet promoting the sales of Liberty Bonds. To further illustrate its patriotic stance, the bank listed five young men working for the bank who had enlisted in the military. Support such as this meant a great deal to customers and patrons as they recognized businesses as patriotic supporters of their community, state and nation. It was a great marketing tool, but more importantly it illustrated the extent to which Americans and business owners supported the war.

In a June 13 article in the *State* newspaper, the sale of Liberty Bonds in South Carolina were reported as being slow at first but gained momentum in the last days of the drive. A final count estimated that South Carolinians purchased $5,075,500 in bonds to support the war. Goals were set for the sale of Liberty Bonds in towns and cities throughout the state. Greenville was expected to amass $335,000, while Spartanburg was expected to reach $200,000. Columbia was expected to reach the $1 million mark, but came up short with only $612,000 from 2,500 subscribers. Lancaster, known for its poor economic climate, was highly successful with over $126,000 raised with the support of workers in the cotton mills. In other regions of the state lower estimates were expected.

All About Liberty Bonds

WHAT Are They?

Liberty Bonds are engraved certificates bearing the guarantee of the Government and People of the United States to repay in gold the full amount loaned, with 4% interest every year.

Liberty Bonds are as safe as the United States.

WHY Should I Buy Them?

Because we are at war. Because we must have dollars as well as men in the fight for freedom. Because every Bond you buy helps to win the war. Because they are the safest investment in the world today.

HOW Can I Buy Them?

For each $50 subscribed pay:
$1 down $20 on December 15, 1917
$9 on November 15, 1917 $20 on January 15, 1918

If you wish, you can buy Liberty Bonds on still easier terms, only $1 down and $1 a week for each $50 Bond at many Banks, Trust Companies, Investment Houses, Stores, etc.

You don't need a bank account to buy a Liberty Bond.

WHERE Can I Buy Them?

At any Bank, Trust Company, Investment Banker, or Department Store.

Every dollar you pay goes to the Government. No commissions are charged to you or paid to anyone.

WHEN Shall I Buy Them?

Buy them NOW. Subscriptions close October 27, 1917.

Our soldiers and sailors will GIVE their lives. You are asked only to LEND your money. If YOU can't fight, your money can. A bond may save a life. A bond will help to end the war.

Buy Your Bonds Today

Publication No. 33

All About Liberty Bonds, unsigned, lithograph on paper, 1917–18. *Courtesy First Liberty Loan.*

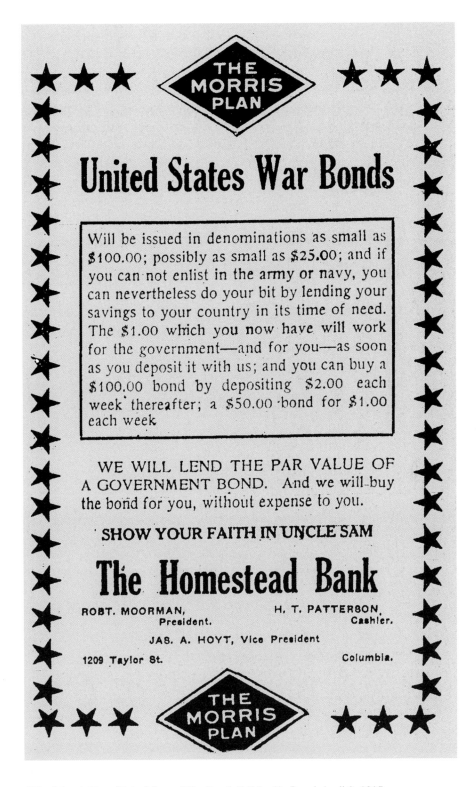

"The Morris Plan: United States War Bonds." *Columbia Record*, April 9, 1917.

Easley, for instance, produced approximately $21,000 in Liberty Bonds, while Conway collected $30,000 and Williamston amassed $15,000.

The sale of Liberty Loans and a Victory Loan was also widely publicized through the production of posters. "For Home and Country" and "Americans All!" were the slogans of posters by Alfred Everitt Orr and Howard Chandler Christy that promoted the sale of the Victory Liberty Loan. "Halt the Hun!" "To Make the World a Decent Place to Live In" and "That Liberty Shall Not Perish from the Earth" by Henry Raleigh, Herbert A. Paus and Joseph Pennell promoted the sale of Liberty Loans. Each of these posters offered a unique glimpse into the marketing techniques of the CPI as artists attempted to reach the sympathies of every American, every South Carolinian.

Remember April 11th, United States Navy Recruiting Day. If you can't enlist yourself get a substitute.
The Loyal Blue Jackets now serving ask you for reenforcement. Do your duty.

Navy Recruiting Day advertisement. *Columbia Record*, April 8, 1917.

WEAR THE
Official Preparedness
Pin 25c
Wiesepape Mfg. Co.
1611 Main Street.

"Wear the Official Preparedness Pin." *Columbia Record*, April 11, 1917.

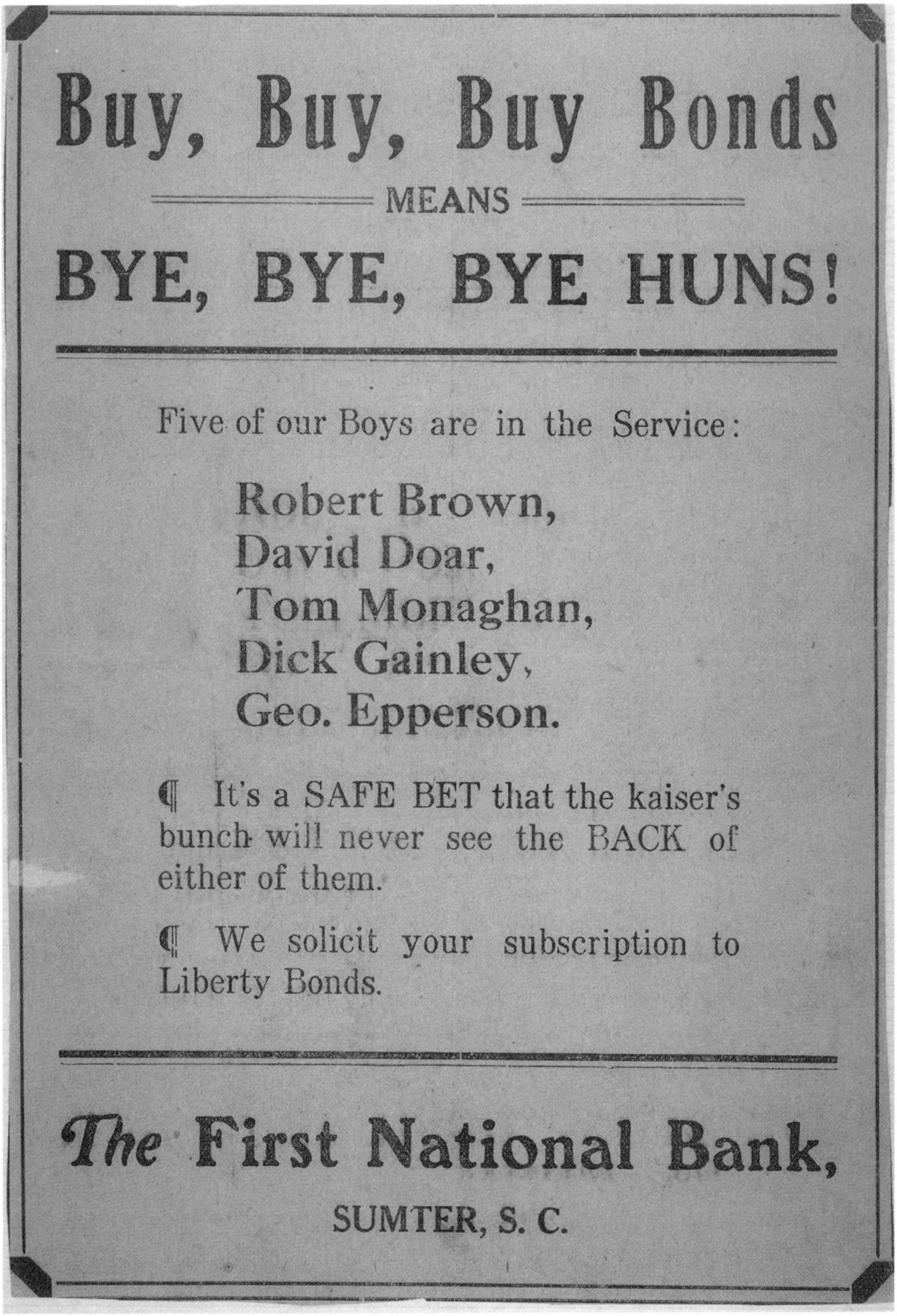

Buy, Buy, Buy Bonds
══ MEANS ══
BYE, BYE, BYE HUNS!

Five of our Boys are in the Service:

Robert Brown,
David Doar,
Tom Monaghan,
Dick Gainley,
Geo. Epperson.

¶ It's a SAFE BET that the kaiser's bunch will never see the BACK of either of them.

¶ We solicit your subscription to Liberty Bonds.

The First National Bank,
SUMTER, S. C.

Buy, Buy, Buy Bonds means Bye, Bye, Bye Huns! Advertisement for sale of Liberty Bonds, the First National Bank, Sumter, South Carolina. *Courtesy South Carolina Confederate Relic Room and Military Museum, on loan from Robert L. Brown.*

143

Haverty-Rustin store advertisement. *Columbia Record*, April 12, 1917.

Newspapers were also successful recruiting tools for the state's military. An ad in the *Columbia Record* on April 3 read, "Will You as Loyal Citizens and Patriots Respond?" The following was the list of requirements for enlistees: "Age 17–30; good teeth; good hearing; good eye-sight; adults must weigh at least 128 pounds and be 64 inches in height; minors must weigh at minimum of 110 pounds at 17 years and be 62 inches; 115 pounds at 18, 120 pounds at 19, 125 at 20."[34] Governor Richard Manning issued a proclamation on the same day designating April 11 as Naval Recruiting Day. The fact that the proclamation was made only three days before the declaration of war was announced suggests that Manning as well as many other government officials knew that war was coming very soon. Of all the military branches, the navy was the most prolific in their advertising for enlistment. Full-page ads in newspapers called for "Young men...who wish to See the World, Save Money, Learn a Trade and Serve Their Country." Recruitment stations were located in Charleston, Florence, Columbia and Greenville.

Sales promotions of merchandise in support of the war also were featured as ads in newspapers. Many local business owners throughout the state offered discounts and specialty items exclusively to those men going overseas. Mimnaugh's Department Store at the corner of Main and Hampton Streets in downtown Columbia took out an ad in the newspaper geared specifically to men in uniform. The store advertised the sale of Munson Army Shoes and that the military had their full support with "prompt deliveries made to Camp Jackson." The State Book Store in Columbia also advertised the sale of military books, including those on trench warfare, officers' and privates' manuals and military field notebooks. The Haverty-Rustin Furniture Company even advertised that purchasing credit with them was as good as the credit the government was establishing to fund the war.[35] An ad in the *Columbia Record* promoted the wearing of the Official Preparedness Pin, sold at the Wiesapape Manufacturing Company store for twenty-five cents. The American Flag and Decorating Co. in Columbia placed an ad in local newspapers emphasizing the sales of United States flags. Tapp's Store promoted the war by giving 1 percent of sales

Honor Button: Liberty Loan, unsigned, lithograph on paper, 1917–18. *Courtesy Victory Liberty Loan.*

PLANT CORN

THE PRESIDENT OF THE UNITED STATES TO FARMERS

"By planting and increasing his production in every way possible, every farmer will perform a labor of patriotism for which he will be recognized as a soldier of the commissary, adding his share to the food supply of his people."—*President Wilson, April 10, 1917.*

Corn must help Win the War

PLANT MORE CORN

PLANT CORN ON ALL SUITABLE LAND NOT USED FOR OTHER FOOD OR FEED CROPS.
IF EARLY PLANTING HAS FAILED, REPLANT WHER-EVER THERE IS A CHANCE FOR A CROP.

THE WINTER WHEAT CROP IS SHORT

Report of May 8 on condition of winter wheat indicates that the crop will be the smallest for 13 years. Condition of spring wheat not yet determined, but estimated wheat production is inadequate to meet prospective demands. More corn will make up for a shortage of wheat.

EAT MORE CORN, LESS WHEAT

 U. S. DEPARTMENT OF AGRICULTURE
WASHINGTON, D. C.
COOPERATING WITH STATE AGRICULTURAL COLLEGES

Above: "United States Flags." *Columbia Record*, April 8, 1917.

Opposite: *Plant Corn*, unsigned, lithograph on paper, 1917–18. *Courtesy U.S. Department of Agriculture.*

during the month of May to the Red Cross to help wounded soldiers and those suffering from the ravages of the war.

National companies such as Victor, the maker of Victrola gramophones and other music machines, promoted their sales by claiming that music would stir every American's patriotism. Wrigley's, the maker of chewing gum, purchased ad space in newspapers drawing attention to the war effort. One ad illustrates a soldier receiving gifts from home that included packs of Wrigley's gum. Welch's, the manufacturer of juices, placed an ad claiming that their product was "The National Drink." The imagery in the ad illustrated the idea that if it is good enough for "our soldiers," it is good enough for the rest of the nation.

Food products were integral to engaging war on behalf of the United States. Before the declaration of war on Germany, Governor Manning made a mass appeal to every South Carolinian to take up the endeavor of producing agricultural foodstuffs to be sent overseas to support the troops in the event it would be needed. His appeal was made not only to the farmers, but also to those living in cities and towns. He asked that they convert backyards and vacant lots into vegetable gardens.[36] Most important were farm-raised crops including corn, peanuts, cowpeas, beans and sweet potatoes. To mobilize this effort, Manning established a campaign committee chaired by D.R. Coker of Hartsville, South Carolina, founder of Coker's Pedigreed Seed Company. Other committee members included E.J. Watson, the commissioner of agriculture in Columbia; Dr. W.W. Long of Clemson College; E.R. Horton of Anderson; and Ira B. Dunlap of Rock Hill. In an

Uncle Sam Needs Leaders of Boys, unsigned, lithograph on paper, 1917–18. *Courtesy Boy Scouts of America, Sacket and Wilhelms Co., New York.*

article in the *Columbia Record*, the Commission for Civic Preparedness made a statement to South Carolinians regarding the preparation of foodstuffs: a "person who does not grow the largest possible amount of food stuffs is helping the enemy of America—Patriotism demands the planting of every available foot in vegetables and truck."[37]

However, Governor Manning's appeal received some opposition—not against the production of agricultural commodities, but against the war. As early as March 31, 1917, in Lexington, South Carolina, a public mass meeting was held regarding the possibility that the United States would enter the European conflict. Representative citizens who conscientiously believed that the United States should not at this time engage in war with Germany convened to raise their voice of opposition to the war. Local farmers supported this movement. Another concern raised was that with the loss of men enlisting in the war, fewer men were at home tending to the production of agricultural products.

A number of Boy Scout groups took up efforts to help with fundraisers, scrap metal drives, Red Cross relief and other activities. In the 1917–18 poster *Uncle Sam Needs Leaders of Boys*, the Boy Scouts were called upon to do their part. South Carolina Scoutmaster

World War I window flag for war service. United States, circa 1914–18. *Collection of Kahal Kadosh Beth Elohim Synagogue, Charleston, South Carolina. Gift of Evelyn Rosenberg Gross-Brien.*

T. Keith Legare of Troop 5 sent a letter to President Wilson expressing the dedication of the Boy Scouts to their community and to the war: "Boys Scouts of America, at Columbia, South Carolina, your boyhood home, offer you their services and assure you of their support and esteem."[38] Legare also sent a letter to Governor Manning expressing similar sentiments.

Patriotism was also illustrated at home in a somber, yet proud manner. Window service flags were issued to the families of active servicemen. The number of family members serving in the military was denoted by the number of blue stars placed on the flag. In Greenville, South Carolina, the Winstock family proudly displayed their service flag for two sons serving in Europe. This overt showing of patriotic support in local communities illustrated the important role that South Carolinians played in both cities and rural towns alike.

Promotion of the Great War was delivered through such diverse formats and methods that nearly every South Carolinian was informed and solicited in some form or another. The government was highly successful in raising support of the war through the creation and efforts of the Committee on Public Information. Local government, industries, communities and individuals all played their part in promoting the war and disseminating information regarding activities on the homefront and the Western Front. The information spread through various channels and methods asking South Carolinians what they, as individuals and as a state, could do to support our nation and our allies. Until the declaration of war on Germany was established on April 6, 1917, South Carolina had not been part of a unified national issue. Thus, for the first time in American history, South Carolinians were called upon to serve the nation in every possible capacity, from taking up arms to fundraising efforts and from the spread of propaganda and educating the public to agricultural preparations for soldiers fighting on foreign soil. In 1917, at the onset of the United States' entry into the war with Germany, South Carolinians took up the effort by answering "a call for all" Americans.

NOTES

Preface

1. For a good synopsis of the current scholarship on the causes of World War I and the resulting devastation to men and territory see Adam Gopnik, "The Big One: Historians Rethink the War to End all Wars," *New Yorker*, August 23, 2004, 78–83. For details on Wilson and his reasoning for going to war see Page Smith, *America Enters the World: A People's History of the Progressive Era and World War I* (New York: Penguin Books, 1985), 441, 504–25.

2. Smith, *America Enters the World*, 540–66.

Seeds of Change: World War I, South Carolina, Impact and Contributions

1. The author wishes to thank the following USC students for their invaluable research assistance for this study: Halie Nowell and Steve Urquart and research assistant Debra Franklin. In addition the author thanks Susan Thoms, local history librarian of the Spartanburg Public Library, for reviewing an earlier draft of this study and providing helpful comments and suggestions.

2. Minute book of the Ladies Benevolent Society of Charleston, South Carolina Historical Society.

3. The phrase "seeds of change" comes from John H. Moore, "Seeds of Change: Charleston and World War I," *South Carolina Historical Magazine* 86, 1985, 39–49; and Theodore Hemmingway, "Prelude to Change: Black Carolinians in the War Years, 1914–1920," *Journal of Negro History* 65 (Summer 1980): 212–27. On the state's farm depression and resurgence see Walter B. Edgar, *South Carolina: A History* (Columbia: University of South Carolina Press, 1998), 481.

4. For Manning's support of Wilson's armed neutrality bill see Boyle W. Boggs, "John Patrick Grace and the Politics of Reform in South Carolina, 1900–1931" (PhD dissertation, University of South Carolina, 1977), 115. On the Zimmerman telegram episode and national reaction

to unrestricted submarine warfare by Germany see Page Smith, *A People's History of the Progressive Era and World War I*, vol. 7 (New York: Penguin Books, 1991), 513–14.

5. *State*, March 5, 1917.

6. Ibid., March 6, 1917; for Greenville see A.V. Huff, *Greenville: A History of a City and County in the SC Piedmont* (Columbia: University of South Carolina Press, 1995), 280.

7. Moore, "Seeds of Change," 39; Boggs, "John Patrick Grace," 111–13.

8. *Charleston American*, April 5, 1917; Boggs, "John Patrick Grace," 108–11.

9. Boggs, "John Patrick Grace," 119–21; Edgar, *South Carolina*, 476–77.

10. Boggs, "John Patrick Grace," 116–17, 119–20.

11. Hemmingway, "Prelude to Change," 215; John Hammond Moore, *Columbia & Richland County: A South Carolina Community, 1970–1990* (Columbia: University of South Carolina, 1993), 377. For the remarks of DuBois on this see *Crisis* 14, no. 1, May 1917, 8.

12. Hemmingway, "Prelude to Change," 215–216, 219; for DuBois's position on the war see *Crisis*, May 1917, 8.

13. Huff, *Greenville*, 280.

14. Moore, "Seeds of Change," 46; Moore, *Columbia & Richland County*, 377, 328; Elizabeth C. West, "Weaving their White Magic: Avenues of Feminine Patriotism in World War I South Carolina" (master's thesis, University of South Carolina, 2002). For the Piedmont story see Richard M. Burts, *Richard I. Manning and the Progressive Movement in SC* (Columbia: University of South Carolina Press, 1974), 165.

15. Moore, *Columbia & Richland County*, 318–19; *50th Anniversary History, 1917–1967, Fort Jackson, S.C.* (1967), 1–2.

16. Moore, *Columbia & Richland County*, 319; William Couper Diary, 1917–1918, Manuscript Collections, South Caroliniana Library, USC.

17. Ibid.

18. Ibid.; *50th Anniversary Fort Jackson*, 6–12.

19. Huff, *Greenville*, 284–85; Alexander C. Doyle, "Completion Report of Camp Sevier, Greenville, S.C." (1917), original on file with U.S. Army Military Institute, Carlisle Army Barracks, PA.

20. Ibid.

21. Susan Turpin, et. al., *When the Soldiers Came to Town: Spartanburg's Camp Wadsworth (1917–1919) and Camp Croft (1941–1945)* (Spartanburg, SC: Hub City Press, 2004), 3–4, 9–18. For a more detailed story of the camp's construction and its short existence see *A History of Spartanburg County* (Band and White, 1940), 236–59 and John C. Edwards, "Doughboys and Spartans: The Story of Camp Wadsworth," *SC History Illustrated* 1, no. 4, November 1970, 4–8, 61–67.

22. Turpin, *Soldiers Came to Town*, 1–6, 57–64; *Survey*, August 18, 1917, 433. On local resentment to outsiders see *History of Spartanburg County*, 250. For price inflation and ways found to resolve them see Edwards, "Doughboys and Spartans," 64–65.

23. Edwards, "Doughboys and Spartans," 65–66; Turpin, *Soldiers Came to Town*, 47–48.

24. Turpin, *Soldiers Came to Town*, 8, 44; *History of Spartanburg County*, 254–55, 246.

25. Fritz Hamer, *Charleston Reborn: A Southern City, Its Navy Yard and World War II* (Charleston: The History Press, 2005), 16; Lawrence S. Rowland, *History of Beaufort County*

(the author wishes to thank Steve Wise of the Parris Island Museum for providing a copy of Professor Rowland's manuscript, which will be part of the forthcoming *History of Beaufort County, Volume II*).

26. Hamer, *Charleston Reborn*, 24; Moore, "Seeds of Change," 39; Boggs, "John Patrick Grace," 111–13; Rowland, *History of Beaufort County*.

27. Moore, "Seeds of Change," 44; *Survey*, August 18, 1917, 435; Jim McNeil, *Charleston's Navy Yard: A Picture History* (Charleston: Coker Craft Press, 1985), 57–65.

28. McNeil, *Charleston's Navy Yard*, 64, 68–69.

29. Moore, "Seeds of Change," 43–44.

30. Eugene Alvarez, *History of Parris Island*, n.d., manuscript copy provided by Parris Island Museum to the author; Rowland, *History of Beaufort County*.

31. Ibid. For descriptions of the Maneuver Grounds and recollections of those who trained there see James Legg, "The Great War at Santa Elena: The Incidental Archaeology of World War One Marine Corps Training on Parris Island, SC" in *In Praise of the Poet Archaeologist: Papers in Honor of Stanley South and his Five Decades of Historical Archaeology*, ed. Linda F. Carnes-McNaughton and Carl Steen (Publications in SC Archaeology no. 1, COSCOPA, 2005), 123–26.

32. *Scuttlebutt & Small Chow: An Irregular Quarterly of the Old Corps, 1898–1941* 1, no. 3, part two, 35, copy provided by the Parris Island Museum.

33. McNeil, *Charleston's Navy Yard*, 65, 66; *State*, November 15, 1917.

34. *History of Spartanburg County*, 248; Rowland, *History of Beaufort County*; Moore, *Columbia & Richland County*, 379.

35. Edgar, *South Carolina*, 477, 481; *Charleston News and Courier*, June 23, 1918. For a general overview of the new prosperity that farmers in the Southeast began to finally realize in the war years see George B. Tindall, *The Emergence of the New South, 1913–1945* (Baton Rouge: Louisiana State University Press, 1983), 60–62. For details about voluntary days without certain foods see Burts, *Richard I. Manning*, 166. For farm income increases see Ernest M. Lander, *A History of SC, 1865–1960* (Columbia: University of South Carolina Press, 1970), 58.

36. Moore, *Columbia & Richland County*, 327, 378; Moore, "Seeds of Change," 44; Huff, *Greenville*, 282; Lander, *History of SC*, 59.

37. Huff, *Greenville*, 283.

38. Moore, *Columbia & Richland County*, 378.

39. Hemmingway, "Prelude to Change," 217.

40. Moore, "Seeds of Change," 44.

41. Terry Helsley, "Voices of Dissent: The Anti-War Movement and the State Council of Defence in South Carolina, 1916–1918" (master's thesis, University of South Carolina, 1974), 73, 75, 76.

42. Ibid., 116, 137.

43. Ibid., 83–84, 88; for the details of La Follette's opposition to U.S. entrance into World War I and the resulting attacks from fellow senators, the press and the general public, see Nancy C. Unger, *Fighting Bob La Follette: The Righteous Reformer* (Chapel Hill: University of North Carolina Press, 2000), 247–50, 253–58, 260–62.

44. Boggs, "John Patrick Grace," 115.

45. Huff, *Greenville*, 282–83; Moore, *Columbia & Richland County*, 327.

46. *Survey*, August 17, 1917, 433; Tindall, *Emergence of the New South*, 54; Moore, "Seeds of Change," 44. For the Spartanburg stories see *History of Spartanburg County*, 244, 247.

47. *State*, November 23 and December 11, 1917, January 19, 1919; Moore, "Seeds of Change," 47–48.

48. *Survey*, August 18, 1917, 434–35; Moore, *Columbia & Richland County*, 324.

49. *Survey*, October 27, 1917, 96; Boggs, "John Patrick Grace," 130; Walter J. Fraser, *Charleston! Charleston!* (Columbia: University of South Carolina Press, 1989), 361.

50. "39th Annual Report of the Executive Committee, State Board of Health," December 1918 (Box 19, Board of Health, Governor RIM Papers, South Carolina Department of Archives and History). On general health problems in South Carolina before and during World War I see Ed Beardsley, *A History of Neglect: Health Care for Blacks and Mill Workers in the Twentieth Century South* (Knoxville: University of Tennessee Press, 1987), 55–58.

51. "39th Annual Report, State Board of Health."

52. *Greenville News*, September 15, 1918; *State*, September 14, 1918; John Barry, *The Great Influenza: The Epic Story of the Deadliest Plague in History* (New York: Penguin Books, 2004), 169–70.

53. Barry, *Great Influenza*, 335–37; *Greenville News*, September 18 and September 22, 1918; *State*, September 19, September 20 and September 21, 1918.

54. McNeil, *Charleston's Navy Yard*, 68–69; Allan D. Charles, "The Influenza Pandemic of 1918–1919 and South Carolina's Response," *Journal of the South Carolina Medical Association* 73 (August 1977): 367, 368–69.

55. Turpin, *Soldiers Came to Town*, 45–46, 50; see Barry, *Great Influenza*, 336–48, for details of this on the national scene.

56. *State*, October 5, 1918.

57. Turpin, *Soldiers Came to Town*, 45–46. For further details on the actual death toll from the flu and its complications afterward see *History of Spartanburg County*, 255–56.

58. For advice on preventing the spread of the disease see *State*, September 21, 1918. For other towns in the state see *Greenville News*, October 9, 1918; Charles, "Influenza Pandemic," 368, 369, 370. For the closing of public facilities and schools see *Greenville News*, October 8, 1918, and Charles, "Influenza Pandemic," 369, 370.

59. Papers of John Wilson Huntley, diary manuscript, at the Manuscript Collection, South Caroliniana Library, University of South Carolina.

60. Petitioners of Ruby, South Carolina (in Chesterfield County) to RIM, D.R. Coker and James H. Haynes, November 22, 1918 (Box 19, Board of Health, Governor Manning Papers, SCDAH); "39th Annual Report, State Board of Health." For details of the county fair that occurred anyway see the *Chesterfield Advertiser*, December 5, 1918.

61. Barry, *Great Influenza*, 396–97; Charles, "Influenza Pandemic," 367.

62. Huff, *Greenville*, 286.

63. Ibid.

64. Rowland, *History of Beaufort County*.

65. Ibid.; Edgar, *South Carolina*, 481–82.

66. For Sevier and Wadsworth closings see *History of Spartanburg County*, 258; Turpin,

Soldiers Came to Town, 72–76. For Camp Jackson's closing see *50ᵗʰ Anniversary, Fort Jackson*, 12–13.

67. Hamer, *Charleston Reborn*, 1–20. For the impact of the Washington Conference on the U.S. Navy ship tonnage and numbers see Smith, *A People's History*, 808–09. For further details about the naval disarmament conference in 1921–22 see David M. Coney, *A Chronology of the U.S. Navy, 1775–1965* (New York: Franklin Watts, Inc., 1965), 238. The five world naval powers in the early postwar era were France, Italy, Great Britain, Japan and the United States.

68. For Gordy romance see Turpin, *Soldiers Came to Town*, 45.

69. Interview with Lois Ann J. Wyly and Reid Wyly, MD, conducted by the author. Summerville, SC, February 23, 1996. The author wishes to thank Katherine Wyly Mille, PhD, Columbia, SC, granddaughter of the Johnstons, for clarifiying exact names and spellings for her grandparents.

70. For the war's impact on women's roles after the armistice see Stanley Coben, ed., *Reform, War, and Reaction: 1912–1932* (Columbia: University of South Carolina Press, 1972), 267–316. For South Carolina and women's suffrage see Smith, *A People's History*, 788, and Edgar, *South Carolina*, 471.

71. Edmund Drago, *Charleston's Avery Center: From Education and Civil Rights to Preserving the African American Experience*, rev., ed. by W. Marvin Dulany (Charleston: The History Press, 2006), 164–65; *Charleston News and Courier*, May 11 and May 12, 1919.

72. Hemmingway, "Prelude to Change," 218–22.

73. Moore, *Columbia & Richland County*, 380; Drago, *Avery Center*, 165–66.

74. *Recollections and Reminiscences, 1861–1865 through the World War*, vol. 9 (SC Division United Daughters of the Confederacy, 1998), 367–68.

"A Wonderful War in Every Way": Columbia during the Great War

1. Margaret Green Devereux, *The Green Girls: A Memoir of our Youth* (Saluda, NC: 1970), 54.

2. *Columbia Record*, April 3, 1917.

3. *Columbia Record*, April 3–5, 1917; "Caroline Girardeau: Custodian of the Confederate Relic Room," *South Carolina Magazine*, January 1951, 58.

4. *Columbia Record*, April 4–11, 1917.

5. John Hammond Moore, *Columbia & Richland County: A South Carolina Community, 1970–1990* (Columbia: University of South Carolina, 1993), 318–19; U.S. Army, *50ᵗʰ Anniversary History, 1917–1967, Fort Jackson History* (Fort Jackson, SC: Army Training Center Infantry, 1967), 4–5.

6. *Fort Jackson History*, 2–4.

7. Moore, *Columbia & Richland County*, 319–20; *Fort Jackson History*, 4. The $12 million figure also includes money spent on a temporary military site north of the city.

8. *Columbia Record*, November 2, 1918.

9. *State*, April 14, 1918; "Caroline Girardeau," 58.

10. Devereux, *Green Girls*, 54.

11. *Columbia Record*, October 2–4, 1917, and November 3, 1918.

12. Ibid., September 28, 1918.

13. Ibid., September 29, 1918.

14. Moore, *Columbia & Richland County*, 324; *Fort Jackson History*, 7.

15. Ibid.; *Columbia Record*, October 5–25, 1918, obituaries; *Columbia Record*, November 2, 1918.

16. *Columbia Record*, November 10–11, 1918.

17. Ibid., March 30, 1919.

18. Ibid., April 3, 1919.

19. *The Jacksonian,* "Home-coming Souvenir Addition," vol. 1 (Columbia: Camp Jackson).

20. Ibid., 10.

21. Moore, *Columbia & Richland County*, 329; "Caroline Girardeau," 58; J.A. Rountree, ed., *The Cross of Military Service ("C.M.S.") Its History and Its Record*, vol. 1 (Birmingham: United Daughters of the Confederacy World War Insignia Committee, 1927), 189. Caroline Girardeau's other son, Claude, joined the American Ambulance Service at age twenty and was cited for bravery in action by the Italian government. Both sons died in their thirties and are buried in Elmwood Cemetery. The Charles J. Girardeau Post of the Veterans of Foreign Wars is still active in Columbia.

22. Moore, *Columbia & Richland County*, 378–81.

23. "World War Memorial Building," National Register of Historic Places Nomination, 1995. The building served a variety of functions through the years. From 1936 through 1960, it housed the South Carolina Historical Commission and the state record collection. During part of this time, the American Legion Auxiliary also used offices on the second floor. The University of South Carolina's Department of International Studies utilized the building from 1960 through 1971. From 1971 through 2002, the South Carolina Confederate Relic Room used the building to display its collection. After 2002, the building has served as office space for various University of South Carolina departments.

24. "World War Memorial Building."

25. Alvin W. Byars, *Olympia Pacific: The Way it Was, 1895–1970* (Professional Printers, Ltd., 1981), 94–95.

26. Byars, *Olympia Pacific*, 94–99.

27. Moore, *Columbia & Richland County*, 323; *Fort Jackson History*, 11; United States Army, "About Fort Jackson, SC," http://www.jackson.army.mil.

28. Devereux, *Green Girls*, 54.

The University of South Carolina in the Great War: Confronting Problems while Contributing to the War Effort

1. William S. Currell to L. Hollingsworth Wood, September 13, 1915, records of the president, 1914–19, University Archives, University of South Carolina.

2. Minutes, board of trustees (BOT), University of South Carolina, June 12, 1916, 186, South Caroliniana Library, University of South Carolina.

3. Daniel W. Hollis, *University of South Carolina*, vol. 1 (Columbia: University of South Carolina Press, 1956), 199, 220.

4. Minutes, BOT, December 12, 1916, 210–11.

5. William S. Currell to Walter W. Haviland, February 3, 1917, records of the president.

6. Minutes, BOT, March 14, 1917, 241.

7. Hollis, *University of South Carolina*, 286–87.

8. SATC information sheet, records of the president.

9. Hollis, *University of South Carolina*, 309–10; Williams S. Currell, *The University and the World War* (Columbia, 1917), 8.

10. Minutes, BOT, April 18, 1917.

11. Hollis, *University of South Carolina*, 287; *Garnet and Black* (Columbia: University of South Carolina, 1918).

12. Oscar Keith to Currell, July 27, 1918, records of the president.

13. Minutes, Clariosophic Literary Society, September 26, 1914, University Archives, University of South Carolina.

14. Ibid., October 2 and October 16, 1915.

15. *Garnet and Black*, 1918.

16. *Carolinian* (Columbia: University of South Carolina, May 1917), 307, (December 1917), 6, (May–June 1918), 48.

17. Ibid., April 1917, 264. The Red Cross trained dogs to carry aid kits to wounded soldiers.

18. *Garnet and Black*, 1918.

19. Ibid.

20. Ibid., 1919.

21. World War I Vertical File, University Archives, University of South Carolina.

22. Hollis, *University of South Carolina*, 289, 292.

23. World War I Vertical File.

24. Hollis, *University of South Carolina*, 289.

25. Ibid., 334.

26. Ibid., 339, 341; four-year report from the president of the University of South Carolina, 1977–81 (Columbia: University of South Carolina), 11.

27. Hollis, *University of South Carolina*, 309–11.

28. University of South Carolina Statistical Profiles, 1981–82 (Columbia: University of South Carolina), 22.

South Carolina Soldiers and Units on the Western Front

1. Robert Elliot Gonzales, *Poems and Paragraphs* (The State Company, 1918), originally appearing in the *State*, circa 1914–16.

2. W.J. Behan, president general of the Confederate States Memorial Association, "A Message to Memorial Women," *Confederate Veteran Magazine*, May 1918, 228.

3. "Caroline Girardeau: Custodian of the Confederate Relic Room," *South Carolina Magazine*, January 1951, 58.

4. C.G. Bierbower, "The Cause Triumphant," *Confederate Veteran Magazine*, March 1918, 131.

5. R.D. Wrights, "The U.D.C. in France," *Confederate Veteran Magazine*, September 1921, 352–3.

6. Martha B. Washington, "An Interesting Letter," *Confederate Veteran Magazine*, August 1918, 370.

7. "The Preparedness Parade," *Confederate Veteran Magazine*, August 1916, 376.

8. Gonzales, *Poems and Paragraphs*, 145.

9. Scrapbook of Sergeant Julius Hubbard, Fifty-seventh Regiment Engineers, 26, unpublished manuscript in the collection of the South Carolina Confederate Relic Room and Military Museum.

10. Scrapbook of Captain Robert T. Brown, 118th Infantry (unpublished manuscript), collection of the South Carolina Confederate Relic Room and Military Museum.

11. "318th Band Is Honored By Nice," *Wildcat* (81st Division newspaper), May 17, 1919.

12. Frank E. Roberts, *The American Foreign Legion: Black Soldiers of the 93rd in WWI* (Annapolis, MD: Naval Institute Press, 2004), 130.

13. Roberts, *American Foreign Legion*, 30.

14. Arthur Little, *From Harlem to the Rhine: The Story of New York's Colored Volunteers* (New York: Covici, Freide; repr., New York: Haskell House, 1974), 146.

15. Joseph Etheredge, "Record in World War of Joseph Oscar Etheredge," *Recollections and Reminiscences 1861–1865 through World War I*, vol. 4 (South Carolina United Daughters of the Confederacy, 1993), 214–15.

16. Captain Walton Chandler, "The 55th Field Artillery Brigade 30th Division" (unpublished manuscript), Colonel William Wallace Lewis papers, South Carolina Confederate Relic Room and Military Museum.

17. Gwen R. Rhodes, *The South Carolina Army National Guard* (Dallas: Taylor Publishing Company, 1988), 41.

18. Ibid.

A Call for All: The Great War Summons the Palmetto State

1. "Lexingtonians to Protest Against War with Germany," *Columbia Record*, April 1, 1917, 1.

2. H.C. (Horace Cornelius) Peterson, *Propaganda for War: The Campaign against American Neutrality, 1914–1917* (Norman: University of Oklahoma Press, 1939), 172.

3. Peterson, *Propaganda for War*, 160–61.

4. Ibid., 162–63.

5. Ibid., 167.

6. "President Will Make His Address Tonight—Wilson Speaks at 8 O'clock," *Columbia Record*, April 2, 1917, 1.

7. Peterson, *Propaganda for War*, 159.

8. Ibid., 169–70.

9. Wayne A. Wiegand, *"An Active Instrument for Propaganda": The American Public Library During World War I* (New York: Greenwood Press, 1989), 53.

10. Stephen Vaughn, *Holding Fast the Inner Lines: Democracy, Nationalism, and the*

Committee on Public Information (Chapel Hill: University of North Carolina Press, 1980), 197.

11. Creel Report: Complete Report of the Chairman of the Committee on Public Information, 1917, 1918, 1919 (New York, 1920), 43.

12. Vaughn, *Holding Fast the Inner Lines*, 149.

13. *Philadelphia Record*, January 27, 1918, 11.

14. Wiegand, *"Active Instrument,"* 53.

15. Ibid., 51.

16. Ibid.

17. Ibid., 46.

18. Vaughn, *Holding Fast the Inner Lines*, 99.

19. Letter from J.W. Searson to Thomas E. Finegan (State Department of Education, Albany, NY), June 5, 1918, CPI Papers; *National School Service* 1 (November 1, 1918).

20. *Columbia Record*, April 5, 1917, 2.

21. Ibid., April 5, 1917, 2.

22. *News and Courier*, April 13, 1917, 3.

23. Vaughn, *Holding Fast the Inner Lines*, 155.

24. Ibid., 116.

25. Committee on Public Information, *Four Minute Man Bulletin* 17, October 8, 1917.

26. Vaughn, *Holding Fast the Inner Lines*, 31.

27. "Colored Women Are Preparing To Do Service," *Columbia Record*, April 8, 1917, 1.

28. Vaughn, *Holding Fast the Inner Lines*, 124.

29. *Columbia Record*, April 4, 1917, 5; "In Alabama, 3 companies of negro volunteers were being organized," *News and Courier*, April 6, 1917, 1.

30. *Columbia Record*, March 28, 1917, 1.

31. Ibid., April 4, 1917, 5.

32. "Patriotic Duty to Prepare Now Officer's Theme," *Columbia Record*, April 1, 1917, 1.

33. Robert L. Brown Collection, The South Carolina Confederate Relic Room and Military Museum, Columbia, South Carolina.

34. *Columbia Record*, April 3, 1917, 10.

35. *State*, August 12, 1917, 17.

36. "Battle Ground of War with Germany are State's Farms," *Columbia Record*, April 4, 1917, 5.

37. *Columbia Record*, April 8, 1917, 10.

38. "Boy Scouts Are Ready for Duty," *Columbia Record*, April 7, 1917, 2.

Visit us at
historypress.net